MEconomy

How to Control Every Part of Your Life

BY

MARK EVANS DM
10X Bestselling Author & Serial Entrepreneur

Ordering Information: Quantity sales. Special discounts are available on quantity purchases by corporations, associations, and others. Orders by U.S. trade bookstores and wholesalers.

ISBN: 9781662916106

www.DreamStartersPublishing.com
DM Publishing Company

Go to MarkEvansDM.com/MEconomy for the chapter my publisher didn't want in the book.

Table of Contents

**Go to MarkEvansDM.com/MEconomy for the chapter my
publisher didn't want in the book.**

Dedication

To my wife Deena and my amazing children Mark III and Dria bear, *without you guys in my life the MEconomy would of never came to life like it did. You inspire me every waking moment to be a better human being and continue on the journey of building the best MEconomy.*

To my parents. *Mom and Dad, I love you more than anything. Thank you for always being there for me.*

And to you. *Yes, you the reader. You're a badass and I'm excited to be on this journey of life with you. I look forward to hearing your MEconomy story.*

The Mission
This book was written to help as many people gain control of their lives as humanly possible. That is why all proceeds are being sent to Tim Ballard's Operation Underground Railroad and various other life-changing charities.

Go to MarkEvansDM.com/MEconomy for the chapter my publisher didn't want in the book.

Foreword by **Sean Whalen**

LIONS™ NOT SHEEP

The only economy is the MEconomy.

You and you alone are the single greatest, and single most valuable economy on earth.

It ain't crypto.
It ain't real estate.
It ain't stocks.

It's YOU.

Without YOU, there is no crypto.
Without YOU, there is no stock market.
Without YOU, there are no REIT's.

Millions of men and women make up the economy.

Millions of people who have money and who've created income compile the stock market investors.

Millions of people who have their own economy (MEconomy) in order enough to invest.

Don't believe me?

The author of this book is a good friend of mine.

He's also a multi-millionaire.

He and I "met" via social media because we both liked cigars. Somehow our paths crossed (thank you mutual friends and algorithms) and we started talking shit via cigars. It was that simple. We both came into each other's space, we both kept adding

5

value (running our MEconomy) and we ended up hanging out on a yacht together.

3 times now.

3 yachts in 3 separate countries to be exact.

Neither of us was In business together. Still to this day we have not "officially" done business together yet we vacation together and hang out regularly.

Here's the reality.

Mark has his economy.

I have my economy.

He ain't worried about mine and I ain't worried about his.

We both wake up every day focused on OUR SHIT (our economy) and that's why we share a friendship and space together.

Could I invest a million with him?

Sure.

Could he invest a million with me?

Yep.

Our personal economies are SOUND and our Intentions every day are focused on our own personal MEconomy, so when we show up in the middle or on a yacht in the islands, our houses are in order and our personal economies (PHYSICAL, MENTAL, EMOTIONAL and FINANCIAL) are in order.

Here's the rub.

Go to MarkEvansDM.com/MEconomy for the chapter my publisher didn't want in the book.

You likely haven't been taught this. Your mom and dad, college professors and educators have shared with you how you're supposed to be a cog in the wheel working for the man for 60 years with the hope that one day you can "retire."

You haven't been taught to be selfish and if you grew up at all in a religious household you've been taught in fact not to be selfish.

I'm gonna tell you why it is the guys like Mark continue to win.

Because he is SELFISH AS FUCK.

Be focuses on HIS PERSONAL ECONOMY FIRST.

That's how he's so charitable.
That's how he's able to give.
That's how he's able to employ people.
That's how he's able to be a friend.

Because HIS ECONOMY is fucking BOOMING!

You think broke people are investing in stocks?

Nope.

You think broke people are donating to small business?

Nope.

You think dad who's working 20 hours a day can be present for his wife and children?

Nope.

This may upset you but the truth is if it does it means you need to hear it.

Go to MarkEvansDM.com/MEconomy for the chapter my publisher didn't want in the book.

You've been lied to for probably all of your life it's time you hear some fucking truth.

YOU MUST BE SELFISH.

YOU MUST GET YOUR HOUSE IN ORDER.

YOU MUST MAKE YOUR ECONOMY BOOM!

Not just to have money.
Not just to hang out on yachts.

But to be truly FREE.

So read this book. Study the hell out of it. Repeat to yourself over and over and over "I AM THE MOST IMPORTANT ECONOMY" then put this book down and invest in that economy like a fucking madman.

You will never regret it.

See you on the yacht,

Sean

Go to MarkEvansDM.com/MEconomy for the chapter my publisher didn't want in the book.

Mark Evans DM & Sean Whalen on yacht trip

Sean Whalen is the founder of multiple companies and a serial entrepreneur. He is also the author of the Amazon bestseller, *How To Make Shit Happen*, which has sold over 425,000 copies. He also coaches other entrepreneurs on scaling their businesses AND their home lives. Whalen is also the founder and CEO of the clothing line, *Lions Not Sheep*.

Go to MarkEvansDM.com/MEconomy for the chapter my publisher didn't want in the book.

Introduction

"There are two things that if you don't have them when you need them, you'll never need them again. A gun and a parachute."

As I sit in my Parkland home, in my cozy office chair, writing to you (with my trusty Glock 9 on my desk), my wife, son and daughter are out back in the pool, enjoying the sun and some music.

We don't have the T.V. on, and we're not paying attention to the news or even social media. Just good ole fashioned hanging out. Later today, we'll talk about our goals, dreams, and where we are right now over dinner.

We know what's going on, and we stay informed, but that's where it starts and stops. Too often, we have more power and control than we think, but outside forces try to manipulate us and control us. When we let them do that, we become pawns to society, the government, media, and fools.

We are halfway through 2021 and the craziness of last year isn't just going to settle down. We have a lot to navigate, and we all have to adjust and always make the best of whatever happens in the world around us. The best way I've

Go to MarkEvansDM.com/MEconomy for the chapter my publisher didn't want in the book.

found to do that is to ignore the outside world and create my own society, culture, and economy.

I call this world my "MEconomy."

We need that proverbial and literal gun and parachute - we have to wrap our minds around protecting ourselves - physically, emotionally, financially - as well as our family. We protect ourselves from free-falls and threats from outside of ourselves. Likewise, we can't run and hide from what's doing us harm - honestly, most of the time, what's doing us the most harm is ourselves.

We can't live in fear, and we have to be ready. We have to be proactive about our health, money, and future; this is the core of the MEconomy.

As I call it, the "ME Economy," or "MEconomy" is often misunderstood. Aren't you living in a bubble when you're living within your own economy? Yes. And, so am I. Everyone is. The only thing you can control in life is you - whether it's the financial decisions you make, the people you invite (or uninvite) to your life, it doesn't matter. The MEconomy is your focus for reality from the moment you wake up. In a nutshell, you need to love yourself, love your family, and build your empire. YOUR empire.

Go to MarkEvansDM.com/MEconomy for the chapter my publisher didn't want in the book.

As we build our empires, we build our confidence - to do more and be more. As our confidence grows, we can better control what we let into our brains and what we let go. For instance, outside news has an agenda, and I guarantee you it doesn't serve YOUR agenda. Instead of comparing yourself to everyone else - your neighbors, friends, competitors, family members - control what you can control and build your own economy.

Let's talk about bubbles for a bit. The biggest criticism I hear when I start talking about this concept of the MEconomy is that living in bubbles is a bad thing and that we should avoid it. Most of the time, we're talking about societal bubbles. Maybe you live in a red, green, blue, or purple political bubble. Or, perhaps you live in an "upper middle class, suburban" bubble. It doesn't matter because I am not talking about that. I'm talking about a "Me Bubble."

The Me Bubble

Here's the thing, we all live in a societal bubble, AND a "Me Bubble." Within whatever group we have chosen to align ourselves (and I'll challenge you on this later), we have other bubbles and environments - workplace, family, neighborhood, friends. But, every bubble pops eventually. The only one you have ANY control over is your environment - your bubble.

Go to MarkEvansDM.com/MEconomy for the chapter my publisher didn't want in the book.

I don't let outside influences affect my drive and focus. Right now, I'm building my businesses, connecting with my kids and family, and during difficult times like living through a worldwide pandemic, opportunities are everywhere (as they always are, if you're aware). We have an amazing opportunity to figure out what's important to us - what it is we want to do, see, and where we want to go in life. Living in this bubble is real, and I love it. I built this bubble. And with each passing day, I'm making it tighter, stronger, more profitable, more healthy.

When we live within our bubble, when we build and focus on **our** *MEconomy*, we aren't thinking about anything or anyone else. We're not worried about the Jones' and how they just bought a new Jaguar (that they can't afford, by the way). We don't care about what our friends had for dinner, or where they've traveled, or their "perfect" life.

"Don't go broke, trying to prove you're not broke to people who are broke."
50cent

Social Media has turned our ability to focus on ourselves inside out. We post what we want others to see, and we see what others want us to see in their posts. It's all false and self-aggrandizing. Social media is so prevalent and

13

ingrained these days. More and more studies have shown how this comparison syndrome can lead to depression.

Sure, there are benefits of social media. We have more access to information and services and people and opportunities that wouldn't otherwise be available to us. Recent studies show a very real correlation between increased social media activity and mental health issues like depression and anxiety, low self-esteem (especially in young adults), insomnia and generally low-quality sleep, and body image problems. The comparison society that we live in, where we think everybody else's life is "perfect," based on what they post, can lead us to believe that we're not good enough.

There is proof that this type of passive social media activity can lead to increased suicide-related thoughts and behavior. We all know about cyberbullying and how it has driven susceptible kids to suicide. Not that long ago, a friend of mine lost a child to suicide. When we focus on others and constantly compare ourselves to other people, we're not putting ourselves first. We're not taking care of or controlling our own world. The young people in our lives need to be supported and taught how to turn their attention inward - and we need to model it.

A parent wrote, after his son's death, "*If you are feeling extreme anxiety, embarrassment, worthlessness, etc., as a*

Go to MarkEvansDM.com/MEconomy for the chapter my publisher didn't want in the book.

result of a shaming attack - close your eyes, and feel it deeply. Let it flood your body for a few minutes until it is fully released. You might cry. Your body may twitch. That's ok. It's a normal part of an extreme release..."

It's very easy to let go of the control we have over our emotions. It's much harder to retain control of our physical and emotional health. We need to teach our kids to use bullying and teasing as fuel to round up their courage and take control of their own lives. We need to teach our kids not to accept being a "victim." We need to show our kids that it doesn't matter what others are doing or saying. First of all, it's none of their business. Secondly, we don't need to compare ourselves to others.

I'm not about to write a textbook on this; just know that this is a symptom of people not focusing on their own lives, their bubble, their MEconomy.

I remember growing up in a small town, and all anyone ever cared about was what so-and-so was doing, who was sleeping with who, who was a drunk, who flunked out of college. I would watch and listen to these wasted lives and realize that I had to be bigger and better than that. I knew that could only happen if I focused inward instead of outward.

Too many of us want others to make decisions for us. We might not even realize this about ourselves. We get stuck in living up to expectations outside our own.

Go to MarkEvansDM.com/MEconomy for the chapter my publisher didn't want in the book.

Dead Dreams

Maybe this will sound like you, and if it does, don't worry. You can reawaken your dreams. But, I see and hear too many people who have become a victim to others. When you're not living in the "MEconomy," you're living in someone else's. You see the world, how they see the world, how they see themselves, and you've given up on your dreams and goals.

You might have a job that, at its core, comes down to you moving a piece of paper from one side of your desk (inbox) to the other side of the desk (outbox) so that you can make the guy in the corner office a ton of money. You're living in his or her economy, not your own.

If you own your own business, and you're working for yourself, you can still be making yourself a victim to others if you're paying too much attention to what's going on outside of your world. Why are we wasting our breath, thoughts, and actions on things that don't serve us? And, that's your new filter - that's how I want you now to see the world.

Does This Serve Me?

We spend too much time and energy on others. We worry too much about what others have and don't have when

16

we need to focus that energy on ourselves. You're in charge. You need to feel that. And you're also accountable for your actions. You're in control of your life and all your economies. Whether those economies are social, business, financial, familial, health...it doesn't matter.

We have only 24 hours in a day - and days are like rechargeable batteries. Either you're doing, saying, or thinking something that charges your battery, or depletes it. You're either spending time with someone who adds energy to your battery or takes from it. If more energy is drained than added, you need to readjust your economies, including social circles, workplaces, and financial economies. You'll know it's the right adjustment for you when you can ask the question:

"Does this serve me?"

It's either a yes or a no. If you fool yourself into thinking/saying, well, maybe, or possibly, or well, neither, you're fooling yourself. There is a lot of gray in the world, but this is black or white. Something or someone is either serving you or not. Something is either charging your batteries or not - if your batteries aren't getting charged, that means they're draining.

Go to MarkEvansDM.com/MEconomy for the chapter my publisher didn't want in the book.

Your Circle

When we were kids, probably in our teens, our parents would tell us to stay away from certain people because they would negatively influence us. Stay away from Matt, or you'll become a druggie, too, or stay away from Alison; she's got no goals in life. If we had a good relationship with our parents and any inkling of good self-esteem, we would heed that advice and carefully choose our friends.

That same advice makes sense when you're an adult, and it's not news that the people that you hang out with the most will influence you - for better or worse. In short, we are the sum of the five people with whom we spend most of our time. If you hang out with people who don't give a crap about what they eat, you won't be as inclined to care either. If you hang out with people who have no real or ambitious goals in life or who are just going through the motions, you are prone to that attitude, too.

I'm not going to sugarcoat it - you become the people with whom you surround yourself. You become your circle. Does your circle lift you up or bring you down? Does your circle have a positive attitude, or do they always think negatively? Everything about life is contagious - the good, the bad, and the ugly. For instance, if you're close to someone who is suffering from severe depression, chances are you will

Go to MarkEvansDM.com/MEconomy for the chapter my publisher didn't want in the book.

catch depression. At the same time, if you're very close to someone who always sees the positive and opportunities in every situation - someone who always says yes to life - then you'll catch that.

Tony Robbins is well-known for making this idea popular, and he states:

"If you take a good hard look at the people you hang around with most, then do some self-reflecting on who you are, you will find you are the average sum of them all — almost as if you carry a little piece of each of them with you."

The idea isn't new. It's something that our parents taught us, and we probably realized, as we got older, that they were right. If we hang out with people who don't have dreams or aren't productive in life, it permits us to be the same. If we hang out with people who don't make excuses about their lives, they'll encourage us not to make excuses about our own lives.

You might also come across people who live in the past - their only victories and accomplishments are from long ago, and they constantly pine for their younger days (the great song by Bruce Springsteen, Glory Days, nails this). I remember chatting with a high school friend I hadn't seen in more than twenty years, and he was still carrying on about

Go to MarkEvansDM.com/MEconomy for the chapter my
publisher didn't want in the book.

high school days and how much he missed it - "Don't you miss those days? Weren't they the best? I'd go back in a second - wouldn't you?"

"Hell no!"

Thinking about and living in the past only drains you - drains your batteries. When you do this, it only means you've given up on being a better version of yourself. If you think you're too old, or that you can't teach an old dog new tricks, I call B.S.! It's not a new trick - it's inside of you. You've just suppressed it, and you haven't really (and honestly) talked with yourself in a while.

Who's This Book For?

My previous books have primarily been about business and entrepreneurship. I built my wealth and reputation mainly in real estate, and I've taught companies how to expand their vision and grow their profits by massive numbers. But, this book is different; I'm writing to a different kind of audience.

I'm writing for my kids. Your kids. Our families and our loved ones. This book is for anyone who feels like there's something, or someone tapping them on the shoulder, whispering in their ear:

Go to MarkEvansDM.com/MEconomy for the chapter my publisher didn't want in the book.

"There's something bigger to life..."

When we hear that voice, we usually don't know what it is. Maybe you're feeling overwhelmed and confused about what life is about or what it could be. It could be that you know you're talking to and listening to and watching the wrong people. You know that you have to stop listening to the media. You have to do something for yourself.

Change is good, but change is hard. But, if you don't change, and don't change your surroundings, your economy, nothing will change. It's like the adage, usually credited to Albert Einstein, "*The definition of insanity is doing the same thing over and over again and expecting a different result.*"

Where you find discomfort in life, you need to change. Where you find comfort, you need to change. And, in this book, I'll help you take steps to make simple and permanent changes that will alter not just how you see the world but manifest in a way that brings about deep, profound change.

Nothing in life is easy unless you have an attitude that everything happens for a reason. I ask you...is life happening to you or for you? and what we have control over is what catapults in either one direction or another.

Go to MarkEvansDM.com/MEconomy for the chapter my
publisher didn't want in the book.

"Never lower your standards, but understand it's your expectations of others that will lead to them disappointing you. You can control your standards. Not theirs."

Mark Evans DM

Go to MarkEvansDM.com/MEconomy for the chapter my publisher didn't want in the book.

Chapter 1

Money

Money is energy. Where you put your energy is where you'll make money. Where you put your money will drive energy your way.

I want to be stupid rich! Let me explain.

If you read this statement and think, "Mark, there's more to life than money," that explains more about you than it does about me. Why? Because it's out of context.

Most people will never financially succeed because they're afraid of being greedy or being perceived as greedy. They think that if someone wants to be rich, they have to take money from someone else - someone deserving - to become wealthy.

What if we live in an economy where if you get wealthier, I get wealthier. If I get wealthier, you get wealthier.

23

Go to MarkEvansDM.com/MEconomy for the chapter my publisher didn't want in the book.

Wealth is not a zero-sum game. We think having money is like sports. That is someone wins, someone loses. The truth is that we all can win because we all have different means, and we all have different goals. Maybe you only want to be worth 10 million dollars, and your friend wants to be worth a billion. In this economy, which we ARE in, by the way, the billionaire can help someone become a multi-millionaire. The multi-millionaire can help someone become a millionaire.

However you define it, how successful you become, is on you. You are responsible for the level of success you achieve, no one else. Go back to the "MEconomy." You and only you can decide your financial objectives, how you'll get there, and the actions you'll take to fulfill your goals.

For me, the number one thing that drives failure in financial success is who you are or are not talking to about your finances. Who are you listening to when it comes to your money? Someone who's a multi-millionaire, where the proof is in the pudding - they've achieved their financial goals? Or someone who's a frustrated cog in the wheel, telling you that you and they will probably always be in debt.

Future Think

Like anything else, to achieve a goal, you have to set a goal. Financial goals, especially, are perfect for this way of

Go to MarkEvansDM.com/MEconomy for the chapter my publisher didn't want in the book.

thinking. I know you know about SMART goals, but let's review them very quickly, so we can move on to where I want to go with this next:

Specific: A goal isn't a goal unless it's REALLY specific. More on this a little later.

Measurable: If a goal isn't a number, it's not measurable. If it's not measurable, how do you know that you're on your way or you've achieved your goal?

Attainable: If your goal is completely unrealistic, you're setting yourself up for failure. Aim high, yes. But, be reasonable.

Relevant: Is your goal relevant to you and others. For example, if your goal is to launch a product, but it's something irrelevant to most of the population - like an automatic toilet paper dispenser - you'll fail. On a personal level, your goal must serve you and whoever else you want it to serve.

Time-bound: Along with measurable, you have to have a specific date or time frame in mind. Example: By August 2025, I want to have $1 million in the bank.

Go to MarkEvansDM.com/MEconomy for the chapter my publisher didn't want in the book.

Since we're talking about money here, I want you to think about something. Where are you right now when it comes to money? How much do you have in cash? How much in debt? How much in investments, including real estate? What's your net worth? What's your monthly cashflow?

Now, I want you to think about where you are now and where you want to be five years from now. Same questions. How much cash do you have? How much debt do you have? What does your investment portfolio looking like? What will your net worth be? How much is coming in monthly?

Drill this down as tightly as you can. Make this specific - in five years, I want to be...

Now you have a measurable and specific goal with a time limit. But wait, is it attainable?

Take a look at where you were five years ago compared to now. Have you made progress? Even if you didn't have a specific goal in mind, have you improved your finances overall, or have they gotten worse? PLEASE don't blame external factors like a bad economy or political uncertainty. Remember, you're living in your MEconomy now.

Be honest with yourself. Own up to everything, good and bad, and take stock of how you've done in the last five years. If your measures have only improved about 5% in five years, you need to make some changes - you're not even

Go to MarkEvansDM.com/MEconomy for the chapter my publisher didn't want in the book.

keeping up with cost-of-living increases. So, either adjust your goal, make huge changes financially (reduce debt, maximize your investments, etc.), and preferably both. So, take stock again - is your five-years-from-now goal attainable? (It may not feel attainable. But you may be feeling a tad overwhelmed writing this number down. It's totally normal as you're putting a number down that's been out there all along it's just now you're focusing on YOUR number and that thing between your ears is starting to seek answers on how to fulfill.)

If it is, let's move on. Is your goal relevant to you and others? Since we're still talking about money, I can't imagine it does not apply to you or your family. Likewise, if your desire is to have $1 million in the bank in five years, more than likely, if you're doing it right, you've helped other people become wealthier, too. Think about it - if you're an entrepreneur in your first year of business, you're on your own most of the time. But, as you grow your business, you have to hire others to help build things out - you're bringing them wealth.

So money is generally pretty relevant, in and of itself. Does it buy happiness? Yes. It makes life a lot easier and more fun. And if you have money, you can help others financially, your church, organizations that help others. You can also take trips and take your family anywhere in the world. Those who say otherwise, have not seen how beneficial money can be for the people and causes that light up your life.

Go to MarkEvansDM.com/MEconomy for the chapter my publisher didn't want in the book.

Your financial objective, your SMART financial goal, is an anchor that you can connect to everything else. Every decision you make will either add to or drain your finances in the long-run. We're not getting any younger. Yes, I know you can improve your health as you age, but you're still aging. Life is finite. No one gets out alive. So, we have to be realistic and make sure we're getting things done while we can, physically and mentally, for ourselves and our loved ones.

One of my friends just found out that his wife's grandmother has no money. Fortunately, he set his finances up so that his family has plenty of money. There is a monthly stipend for his family member so that she doesn't have to worry about finances anymore. He set up his life, so he's got the resources to help out a family member and doesn't even have to blink. Again, as we create wealth for ourselves, we can create wealth for others. Folks that say, "Money doesn't buy happiness" simply haven't given enough away to others who need it.

Options

When you're wealthy, you have options that aren't normally available. Picture this - as I'm writing this book, we're in the middle of a worldwide pandemic. If you only have $15 in the bank, and you're about to lose your job, you may have

Go to MarkEvansDM.com/MEconomy for the chapter my publisher didn't want in the book.

been barely getting by when things were good. This type of situation WILL play out again - things that are out of your control, yet you have more control than you think.

When you've set your life up for wealth, you have money and options for when things change - and we all know that change is a basic fundamental of life. Life is changing. So, when something like a worldwide pandemic hits, for instance, you've got options. You can hunker down and stay safe - working from home, spending time on a property you bought, so you can relax with the kids and go hiking or fishing.

If you have money, you can head out in an ultra-luxurious R.V. and travel the country, unencumbered. You can buy a luxury sailing yacht and sail around the world. Maybe you want to build a self-sustaining compound where you're not even worried about being tied to an outside power source. It doesn't matter. The bottom line is that it takes money to do this - it takes money to build and create your life options for you and your family.

This reality comes from preparation - from future think. It buys you options, and it buys you time to ride it out when times get tough in the world. This is all that money does. People think money is the end result. But the end result of wealth, of money, is to have options. With these options, you can help those you care about, the people close to you.

Go to MarkEvansDM.com/MEconomy for the chapter my publisher didn't want in the book.

There's no better feeling for me than to hand my sister keys to a brand-new car. I have that option.

But with that said, your world doesn't have to be tough. Look around. Who's struggling the most right now? The ones who aren't prepared. The ones who didn't get their finances in order. Truth is no one taught you this shit. If formal education is so amazing, why are all these folks broke? Why do they have their hand out for a check from the government? We must open our eyes and look at this through a new lens. If you're struggling with money, it's YOUR fault. No one else's. Great news is you're here and learning how to get your things in order.

Where I come from, a small town in Ohio, people were barely making it. I didn't know anyone making over $100,000 a year until I left that area and went on to pursue my own life - build my economy. That became my goal, back in 1996 - to clear $100,000. That, to me, with my background, was like saying I wanted to be a millionaire. Keep in mind, I barely graduate high school, and never went to college since it wasn't even a thought for me.

The mentality of where and when I grew up was that if someone drove up in a cool, new car, they must have ripped off or scammed someone to get that car, or that new house, or expensive vacation - whatever - it didn't matter. The thought process that to make money, you had to hurt someone else was prevalent and still is today.

What I discovered, though, that the vast majority of wealthy people are very nice, giving people. They made their money honestly and through hard work and a little luck. Most of them have failed - miserably - sometimes losing everything. But, no matter what, they never lost sight of their goal. Maybe achieving it got delayed, but the vision was always there. Their "why" was strong enough to survive any speed bump. Their eye was on the prize.

Find these people and talk to them. Learn from them. They might have some ideas for you and give you an opportunity that you wouldn't have otherwise. It really is about who you know, and building relationships with people you want to be like is vital to finding your path and creating your economy.

You have to educate yourself about financial literacy. Finance is not typically taught in schools and very few homes. According to Youth.gov, between 2004 and 2009, credit card debt among college students rose almost 75%. Only half of the high-school kids tested passed a test of financial literacy. In a National Longitudinal Survey of Youth, just a quarter of teens knew what inflation was and could calculate simple interest rates. This last holiday season, in the middle of the

Go to MarkEvansDM.com/MEconomy for the chapter my publisher didn't want in the book.

pandemic, one-third of Americans went into debt to buy Christmas gifts.

If you're a parent, this is your responsibility. By not teaching financial responsibility and literacy, you're coddling your kids, and you're protecting them from reality. When, in fact, if we withhold money from our kids, so they earn and learn on their own, and teach them what we know about saving, investing, debt management, and earning potential, we are sending them out into the world more likely to succeed.

It's ok to suffer. I was talking recently to a young adult (he was 22 at the time) who had convinced themselves that they had to build a "nest-egg" before they would leave their parents' home. "Dude, leave…" I told him.

So what if he had to live in a studio or tiny one-bedroom apartment until he could make enough money to upgrade his life? Those are great times. Living through adversity and scrimping and saving is what teaches you financial literacy. Sure, you can read it in a book, but nothing is a better teacher than reality. That's where you figure out what you're made of, to see if you're prepared for the "storms" of life.

Go to MarkEvansDM.com/MEconomy for the chapter my publisher didn't want in the book.

Taking Control

You control your opportunities. You control who you decide to work for (and with), your investments, savings habits, and debt-to-income ratio. You control what and when you buy and how you spend your money. You control what type of car you drive, what house you live in, your chosen neighborhood. You control how you spend your money for leisure and luxury.

The mindset around money starts and ends with you - you have 100% control over these decisions. Even if things change around you, you control how you will respond, financially and otherwise.

You control you. You control your money. Don't blame mom or dad who told you that you had to be an accountant, lawyer, or a doctor. You're an adult now. If those paths others want you to take aren't cutting it for you, you have to take another turn. Live for yourself - not for your mom or dad, or anyone else. If you're not living for yourself, first and foremost, you're not living at your highest capabilities. If you're more worried about what your parents, friends, or colleagues think of you, you won't be making decisions that serve you and your own family.

You also can take control of your past. Many of you have experienced horrible things in your life - and you can

Go to MarkEvansDM.com/MEconomy for the chapter my publisher didn't want in the book.

control how you use that past to guide your future. If you keep using your past to cause heartache, financial stress, or anything else negative in your life, that's on you - and not the person who harmed you. I'm not saying this is easy, by any stretch. But, you can take control of your past, your present, and your future.

Until you've taken this control, you're always going to be a victim: victim or victor, it's your choice. When you've accepted being a victim, you'll never live to your greatest potential, and deep down inside, you know you are missing out. You don't wake up a millionaire with everything figured out. But, you can wake up to the knowledge that this is a journey. Catch some winds. Invest a few minutes every day reading about financial literacy. Spend a little time every day learning a new skill. Get a start on your way. Get those wins under your belt.

Too often, we judge those who make these choices to have nice cars, a nice house, to make a ton of money. What others think about us doesn't matter. If your moral compass is strong, your wealth will come and can be shared with others. That's all that matters. That you have a plan and you work the plan.

Go to MarkEvansDM.com/MEconomy for the chapter my publisher didn't want in the book.

Investing in Ourselves

If we have the means, we'll do anything for our kids that we can afford, and sometimes what we can't afford. For instance, let's say that your kid is pretty good at a sport, and they want to pursue it. You hire them a coach or teacher to help them through. If they're struggling in school, you hire them a teacher or tutor. If they want to learn to play the piano, you hire them a piano teacher.

So, why don't we do this for ourselves? When we need help or want to learn something new or pursue a hobby or passion, there's nothing wrong with spending money to invest in ourselves. If you know you need help getting your business on track, it's a power move; it's a strong move to ask for help and hire a coach. If you know you need help staying on track to be healthy, you're showing that you care about yourself when you hire a trainer or a health coach. You're investing in yourself. And, that is money well spent and the best investment you could ever make.

We've been programmed not to ask for help; that it's a weakness. We've been conditioned to buck up and get it done by ourselves. But, we have to realize that now is the time. We don't know how much time we'll have on this planet. We don't know how much time we'll have with our kids, with our parents. When we ask for help to develop our own skills and

Go to MarkEvansDM.com/MEconomy for the chapter my publisher didn't want in the book.

potential, we are creating a future where the time we have left is of a higher quality, where we're more conscious of what we have, what we need, and who we value.

Go to MarkEvansDM.com/MEconomy for the chapter my publisher didn't want in the book.

Chapter 2

Time

When I talk about wealth and being stupid rich, I am not thinking solely of money. I'm also thinking about the concept of time. I want to be a time-illionaire. Time is what life is made of; we count time. We live in different time zones, and we watch time pass. The time we spend with our family or friends is invaluable. The time we spend working to make monetary wealth is what we trade for attaining that wealth.

Think about the cost of everyday items, like a cup of coffee at Starbucks. If you're working at an entry-level job, you might be bringing in $12-15/hr. So, a $5 cup of coffee is equal to 20 minutes of your time. You're trading that time, and the money you earned during that time, to buy that cup of coffee. I'm not saying that you shouldn't enjoy your coffee, but maybe the trade-off isn't worth it. Suppose you're only making $15/hr.

Go to MarkEvansDM.com/MEconomy for the chapter my publisher didn't want in the book.

and you spend $5 on a cup of coffee. You've just traded 1/3 of your time in that one hour to pay for that coffee. Is it worth it to you?

The time I get to spend with my kids is worth it to me - the time I can spend with them in twenty years is even more valuable to me. Why? Because in twenty years, that much time will have passed, and that will mean that I have twenty years less time to spend with them. As we get older, time becomes more valuable. Many of us don't want to grow old. If we do manage to get old and gray, we're the lucky ones. Many don't make it that long. Time is valuable, and we need to treat it like a treasure.

We've been taught a lie about retirement. You're sacrificing your time working today with the hope that in 30 years, an hour will be worth the same as it is now. What happens when you finally retire, but you're unhealthy, or you're in a wheelchair? What if you never get the chance to retire?

I'm not saying you shouldn't work. I'm saying that you should be more conscious of what you're building and why. Me? I want more time.

As my parents get older - I want more time with them. If we're lucky, given life span averages, I might have ten years more with them. That sounds like a lot of time, but it's only ten

Go to MarkEvansDM.com/MEconomy for the chapter my publisher didn't want in the book.

birthdays. It's only ten Christmases. It's only ten summers. As we all know, the days drag on, and the years fly by.

If I'm sitting here, planning twenty years out into my future, more than likely, my parents will be gone. So, here's the problem. I see it everywhere. If you're not keeping an eye on your time account, as much as you look at your bank account, you're missing out.

The MEconomy and Time

In the last chapter, we looked at the money in the "MEconomy. You can almost read the chapter and substitute time for money or wealth. However, I want to talk about some specifics here. Just like you have to invest money for your future, you also have to invest time. Are you spending your time wisely? When you spend time, time away from your family, is it for a bigger purpose? Will it buy you more time down the line?

Life isn't about surviving. It's about living and thriving while you're alive. It's incredibly important to put your time and energy behind the things that matter to you and your loved ones. When you consider that time is energy, and energy is time, you can see how the MEconomy demands that your time - your energy - is spent on only things that serve you, on

Go to MarkEvansDM.com/MEconomy for the chapter my publisher didn't want in the book.

only people who give you time and energy. It always comes down to this.

"The key is in not spending time, but in investing it."
Stephen R. Covey.

Time as an Investment

How do you spend your time? When you're at home or work, is your time spent on important or fulfilling things? Is your time spent primarily on things that serve you and your potential - something that will create and build your "MEconomy?" A recent Gallup study found that more than 300,000 of those surveyed spent almost half of their time on unimportant things - busy work.

They wasted almost half of their time on trivial and unimportant activities. But, I get it. We're often juggling a lot of different things. Maybe you're overwhelmed and stressed out - perhaps you think you're working on important things, but you're really not. When you're spending time this way, it's like you're on a gerbil wheel—running as fast as you can to get nowhere. It feels like you're doing something because you're exhausted at the end of the day. It might even feel like it's important because you're just so busy all day.

On the surface, it isn't necessarily a terrible thing. But to me, it's tragic. When you're spinning on the wheel, you're

Go to MarkEvansDM.com/MEconomy for the chapter my publisher didn't want in the book.

spending time doing things that just don't matter. And that leaves little, if any time, to work on big goals - to be creative - to build your "MEconomy." You're spinning wheels for someone else, or if you work for yourself, you're working in your business rather than on your business.

Blame Your Brain

To build new momentum, stop the wheel. Literally pause what you're doing and reorient yourself. Look around and take inventory of how you feel and what's driving you. What is taking up your mental space? What consumes most of your emotional energy?

Observe where and how you're spending your time and measure it against what you really want. Spinning your wheels simply means you either don't know what you want or you don't have the knowledge or skill set to effectively get to where you want to go.

Closely monitor your actions and habits, and constantly ask, "Is this activity moving me forward and closer to my goal?" If not, eliminate what's not working now and replace it with something that will. Get through the action to create new traction.

Go to MarkEvansDM.com/MEconomy for the chapter my publisher didn't want in the book.

Every new energy and step will now allow you to move forward instead of being worn out going in circles, with less energy and more results.

Two Brains

Obviously, I'm not a neuroscientist, and this is an incredible simplification of the brain. But I think it's worth looking at how we are hard-wired to spend time the way we do. The good news is that your brain can be retrained to do something different like any muscle in your body.

Basically, we have two brains - the ancient or more primitive part of our brain and the more refined and developed part of our brain. The older part of the brain is our "reactive" gray matter. It is the part of the brain that controls the fight or flight mechanism. Like when ancient peoples literally had to escape what it was threatening them - like the proverbial Sabre-toothed tiger chasing the hunters. The threat triggers the primitive brain to react so we have a better chance to survive a physical threat. It allows us to survive, and it's worked to get us this far in humanity. The problem is that this is purely reactive - not a lot of thought or reflection happens here.

Good thing we have the thinking part of the brain that gives us the ability to reflect on what's happening around us

Go to MarkEvansDM.com/MEconomy for the chapter my publisher didn't want in the book.

and to make carefully considered decisions. Here is where we're better able to analyze how we want to spend our time. The problem is that the reactive brain, the survival brain, is very strong. And if we're stressed out or upset, that part of the brain takes over. We react instead of thinking. And when we stop thinking, we stop spending our time wisely.

Our brain actually tricks us. Because when faced with important things to do, things that require our thinking brain, our reactive brain is triggered instead. So, we tend to rush through those things without even giving them much thought. We look back on the day and say, "wow, I was productive today."

Were you, though? Were you really consciously aware of what you did that day - did it leave your thinking brain available to give more thought and time to things that might have been more important? Are you addicted to the sense of urgency that your reactive brain feeds? Just because something feels like it's urgent or critical, is it?

Dopamine, or the feel-good neurotransmitter, almost acts like a drug. When you've been running around like a chicken with your head off all day, and you get things done, dopamine is released. We like feeling that we're productive. It tricks us into thinking that it's adding energy, and our brain feeds this by producing more dopamine. But, after the "rush" of busywork, we can look back with our thinking brain and

Go to MarkEvansDM.com/MEconomy for the chapter my publisher didn't want in the book.

realize that we've wasted time on the mundane details versus investing time on bigger and more important things.

Stephen Covey and Time Management

You have probably heard of Covey and his Time Management Matrix. I think this is an incredibly effective tool to help us use our thinking brains to stay out of reactive mode AND train ourselves to make better decisions about what's important to tackle next.

Within this matrix, you can categorize your time based on urgency versus importance - remember, those two things aren't the same. Something can be very urgent, but not important - trivial. At the same time, something can be very important, but not urgent. Although Covey had day-to-day business and work tasks in mind when he developed this matrix, I think you can use it in a much broader sense.

Instead of thinking about the Covey quadrants in the context of tasks, think of them in relation to your "MEconomy" and how you want and need to spend your time. We can use Covey's simple tool for complex life questions. To understand how to prioritize our time to build our best potential self. Most are so busy making money today that they don't have time to get wealthy.

Go to MarkEvansDM.com/MEconomy for the chapter my publisher didn't want in the book.

Apologies to Covey, but here's his Time Management Matrix adapted for our discussion:

	Urgent	**Not Urgent**
Important	*Quadrant 1: Necessity* Critical and immediate tasks Last-minute obligations	*Quadrant 2: Extraordinary Productivity* Long-term goal setting Strategic planning Relationships
Not Important	*Quadrant 3: Distraction* Busy-work (emails, calls, minor issues) Questions from others	*Quadrant 4: Waste* Routine tasks and chores Chit-chat Killing Time

Necessity - Quadrant 1

We need to do this stuff because we can experience some pretty serious consequences if we don't. In the "MEconomy," this quadrant means we're taking care of things that come up that might take us away from our comfort zone, but they're important and urgent. Let's say you're on vacation, getting some needed down-time, but you get a call from a

45

family member that your mom or dad is very sick. You need to go. You have to go, and it is time well spent, even as it interrupts important relaxation time.

Extraordinary Productivity - Quadrant 2

It's tempting to put this stuff off, but this quadrant, I think, is the most important. Since these types of things are not urgent, they might not seem important. But they're the most important, and the best place to spend your time. You're thinking of the big picture, planning for the future, putting things in play for ten, twenty, thirty years down the line. You're working on relationships - taking care and nurturing relationships with people who are there to help and support you and who could even help you down the line. You should spend most of your time here. Right here is the core of the "MEconomy!"

Distraction - Quadrant 3

The vast majority of us spend the vast majority of our time distracted and doing busy work. You're running on the gerbil wheel but not moving. These are distractions. Now, realistically, you can't avoid them altogether, but you can minimize your time here. The easiest way is to delegate them

Go to MarkEvansDM.com/MEconomy for the chapter my publisher didn't want in the book.

out. If you can't do that, dedicate one hour in the morning to answer your emails, instead of letting those messages distract you throughout the day. Don't get sucked into answering an Instant Message instantly - very rarely is that necessary. Get your more important work done, then pay attention to these little things that can truly wait.

Waste - Quadrant 4

Before I carry on about this quadrant, I want to state that I know that down-time is important. Actually, it's critical. But, I see too many people spending *way* too much time here. I'm a go-getter. I could probably spend more time on the wasted-time category. But I can't tell you how many times people have said to me, "How do you get all that done?"

Yet, if they were to look at their own lives, they would see that they're wasting time watching T.V., playing video games, surfing and scrolling on social media, memorizing sporting team and player stats. This time and energy are wasted and go from constructive to destructive. There's a fine line between these two. Wasted time you enjoy isn't wasted. On the other hand, wasted time that uses up productive MEconomy time is most certainly wasted.

Go to MarkEvansDM.com/MEconomy for the chapter my publisher didn't want in the book.

Focus on What's Really Important

Only you can decide what's truly important to you. But, don't be tricked and lulled into being a pawn to your society, to the media, or what you think other people expect of you. How you spend your time is a direct reflection of your ability to take care of yourself and those around you. If you're spending time in a way that keeps you "in place," you can retrain your brain to use your thinking brain more than your reaction brain.

Here are some tips that might help:

Control Your Emotions - use your thinking brain and make rational decisions rather than emotional ones. Meditate and keep yourself calm.

Stay Mindful - when you're stressed - stop. Reflect instead of reacting. I think we all have a superpower within us, and that's to feel grateful when we're stressed and overwhelmed. Gratitude can change the attitude.

Organize Your Time - use the modified Covey Time Management Matrix. Focus on Quadrant 2 tasks.

Go to MarkEvansDM.com/MEconomy for the chapter my publisher didn't want in the book.

Analyze - Track your time for a month. Where are you spending your time, and how much time are you spending in Q2 versus Q4, for example? Many time management apps can help you do this.

Just Say "No!" - If you find yourself too often in Quadrants 1 and 3, learn to say no whenever you can. You usually don't have to explain yourself, but if you do, use the language of the matrix - "I can't because it's not really urgent or important..." Take no prisoners; this is YOUR economy and your time.

It's not how much you checked-off your "to-do" list at the end of the day - that doesn't define productivity. That only reveals how "busy" you were. Instead, use your thinking brain to decide what's important and how to spend your time. Sometimes that means that you're avoiding work time to spend time with your family. Sometimes that means you're spending less time with your family today so that you can build a life that allows you to spend many more hours every day with them.

Go to MarkEvansDM.com/MEconomy for the chapter my publisher didn't want in the book.

Chapter 3

Health

"I am my greatest asset. I am my greatest investment. Me. My mind. My skill set. My body. My emotional health. My mental health. My physical health."

Mark Evans DM

Health truly is the key to everything. Without health, I don't think you can truly have happiness. Likewise, without happiness, I don't think you can have health; the two are inextricably linked.

With good health, we have more options, just like with money. You can do more when you are in good health. You have more energy to work on your business. You have the physical strength you need to pursue hobbies and adventures. If you want to sail around the world, you need to be healthy.

Go to MarkEvansDM.com/MEconomy for the chapter my publisher didn't want in the book.

For example, boats are not designed for overweight, out of shape people. Your health will drive your dreams.

But, let me make this clear. Health doesn't mean being on the latest fad diet or taking the latest fad supplement. Health is a state of mind, and the longest-lived people on the planet focus not on exercise routines but an active lifestyle. They move a lot. They don't drive anywhere or have tools that automate every aspect of their lives. Their lives are built around movement. Sitting on the floor in Okinawa, Japan, throughout the day, exercising by getting up and down off the floor dozens of times a day. Other long-lived populations do everything by hand-building fences, landscaping, and you name it. They also eat whole, seasonal foods, have strong social networks, and worship. If you're looking to live healthily well into your 90s, you probably need to change your habits, which doesn't mean just buying a home gym.

Full disclosure is an aspect of my life where I struggle the most. By no means am I a health expert, but like most of us, I have things in my life that I need to work on. And health is definitely one of those things for me. I know I need to eat better and less. When I feel like I'm getting into the slumps, health-wise, I have to jolt myself and get down to reality. I have to force myself to get on the scale - the same piece of equipment I've been staring at for the last thirty days. But

Go to MarkEvansDM.com/MEconomy for the chapter my publisher didn't want in the book.

every day, I'm working on this, and am finding more motivation. I'm getting healthier and healthier.

We all suppress things. But, we can't suppress our health. Sooner or later, if we're not taking care of ourselves, our health will fail faster than it needs to and quicker than we're programmed. But the whole concept of the MEconomy is that we accept responsibility for our actions. We have 100 percent control over what we put in our mouths, how we move throughout the day, and how we build and nurture our health.

But when it comes down to it, it's pretty simple. You're either on a path toward better health or a path toward worsening health. We can't make ourselves younger, and we can't go back in time. But we can put ourselves on a healthier road to be around for our loved ones, tap into our full creativity and energy, and live our fullest MEconomy life.

I've worked with many entrepreneurs, and the most consistent thing about us is how inconsistent we are. So, as we're building our health, that's usually our downfall. As we're building our businesses and our life, we take certain priorities and put other things to the side - and, often, that means our health. I'm not judging that - as I said, this is something I know I can be better at than I am right now.

Sometimes all we need to do is pay attention, notice our habits and how they affect our health, and then do something about it. There are 1000s of programs under the

Go to MarkEvansDM.com/MEconomy for the chapter my publisher didn't want in the book.

sun, and there may be one there for you. Again, overall health isn't just about diet and exercise; it's much more complex and interesting than that.

I'm in better health today than I was ten years ago, and I'll be in better shape in ten years from now. It didn't happen by any "massive" action, but by taking forward steps toward optimal health.

Mental Health

Our mental health might be the most difficult aspect to nurture. We often put our mental health into a mental health professional's hands, and there is most definitely a time and place for that. At the same time, I think there are many things we can do for ourselves in this regard. Like physical health, I don't think you can be truly happy unless your mental health is optimal.

And let's talk about this term, "optimal." We often talk about "healthy" as the absence of disease. But, I think health, physical, emotional, spiritual, and mental, is more than just the absence of apparent problems. We should think more in the sense of optimal health. So, in this context of mental health, it wouldn't just mean that you're "ok," it would mean that you're optimally healthy - you're thriving.

Go to MarkEvansDM.com/MEconomy for the chapter my publisher didn't want in the book.

Again, I'm not the professional here - just an observer. I've been through many, many lows and many, many highs. If you're optimally mentally healthy, you can get through difficult times a little easier. That's not to say hard times are easy - they're not. But when we think of the MEconomy, and focusing on the things that serve us, that allow us to be the best person we can be, we have to focus on our health in all aspects. Like every bone and system in the body is connected within a whole, so is our health.

A question I get ALL the time is, "Mark I have ADHD - how do you deal with it?"

Truth is I think most if not everyone could be labeled as a person that has ADHD. First off, why do we think this is a bad thing having ADHD? I truly believe it's a superpower, if you know how to harness it correctly.

Too many folks get labeled and believe things without researching. They start popping pills to suppress one's "superpower," and those pills turn them into zombies.

With the world we live in, most, if not all of us have a form of ADHD. The drug makers love this. Learn how to harness the power of ADHD and enjoy the journey.

Go to MarkEvansDM.com/MEconomy for the chapter my publisher didn't want in the book.

Living Long, Living Healthy

In the early 2000s, National Geographic and other organizations asked journalist Dan Buettner, a long-distance cyclist, and a National Geographic fellow, to research and explore the world's longest-lived populations. Five locations where the highest percentage of centenarians lived were identified - and Dan, along with other researchers, delved into what they had in common. Their research took them to California, Costa Rica, Japan, Greece, and Italy. (www.bluezones.com)

The researchers call these places **Blue-Zones**. Through community visits, interviews, dietary and habit studies, nine common behaviors were identified between these very diverse populations. Each of these behaviors fits in beautifully with the health aspect of the MEconomy, as you'll see:

Move Naturally - as mentioned previously. Instead of pumping iron or joining gyms, the world's longest-lived people move without planning or even thinking about it. They live in places where they can walk to visit friends or go to the store. They walk to church (more on that later), and many of them have gardens that they tend to manually.

Go to MarkEvansDM.com/MEconomy for the chapter my publisher didn't want in the book.

If you don't live in such a place, you'll have to think about it more than these folks do. Make things a little inconvenient - take the stairs, park far away, skip the moving walkway or escalator, walk your dog, get rid of time-saving electronics and power equipment that allow you to be lazy. Sure - go to the gym. No harm done - but, more importantly, structure your life to MOVE!

Your Why - What's your sense of purpose? What's your why? If you know the answer to that question, I'm going to challenge you a little bit. Ask yourself what your purpose is, your why? Now, ask that again. What's that answer? Now ask, 'Why?' again. Do this for at least four or five "whys."

In Okinawa, this knowledge is called ikigai, and in Italy, plan de Vida. Both roughly translate into "why I wake up in the morning." Why do you wake up in the morning? Take inventory of your life. What are your passions, talents, gifts? What are things you love to do, people you love to be around? Why? When you know these answers, you'll be able to build your purpose for your MEconomy with deliberate action, words, and feelings that you have 100 percent control over.

Relax - We are all under stress, all the time. Some of this stress is real, and a lot of it is imaginary. When you're

Go to MarkEvansDM.com/MEconomy for the chapter my publisher didn't want in the book.

emotionally or physically stressed, your body doesn't know the difference. It still senses that you're under attack, triggering your fight or flight response. This kind of response leads to chronic inflammation - heart disease, cancer, and auto-immune conditions are all linked to inflammation.

In Okinawa, Japan, they take time every day to reflect on their life and remember and honor their ancestors. Seventh-Day Adventists in Loma Linda, California, pray. In Italy, Sardinians have a drink with friends, enjoying a locally made wine. You can down-shift by taking a nap, meditating, taking a walk, praying, or partaking in a relaxing hobby like painting, reading, or writing. The important thing is to make it a daily habit.

80% Rule - We eat too much. Portion sizes in the United States have increased by 100% from 50 years ago. Instead of eating until you're full, push yourself away from food when you're 80% full. Why? Because it takes about 20 minutes for the "I'm full" signal to reach our brains. By the time it does, we've already overeaten.

The Confucian mantra, Hara Hachi bu, reminds Okinawans to stop eating before they're full. A person says it before the meal. You can also naturally eat less by using smaller plates, not watching T.V., and being acutely aware of what you're eating while you're eating it. In general, Blue Zones populations eat the smallest meal of the day in the early evening and then don't eat for the rest of the day. Food for thought.

Mostly Plants - Most of the longest-lived populations aren't strict vegetarians or vegans, except for the Seventh Day Adventists. However, in general, meat products' consumption is limited to once a week, and dairy is limited, including eggs. Their diet is mostly fresh fruits and vegetables, beans, lots of green leafy veggies, and other disease-fighting foodstuffs like nuts, seeds, and whole grains.

Instead of following the latest fad diet to lose weight or get in shape, push yourself away from your small plate of whole, healthy foods. We know this. I mean, this all makes sense, right? If you're going to eat meat, (I love and eat a lot of meat) make it a condiment and not a 16 oz slab of beef on your plate. Have a nice cut, really enjoy it, savor it, and then focus on healthier options for the rest of the week.

Evening Drink - Here's one most of us can get behind. Except for the Seventh Day Adventists, who don't consume alcohol, each of the Blue Zone populations enjoy limited drinking in social situations without overdoing it. Red wine is

Go to MarkEvansDM.com/MEconomy for the chapter my publisher didn't want in the book.

beneficial since it's loaded with antioxidants and reduces certain cancers and heart disease risk. So, one glass for women and two for men.

Build Your Tribe - This concept was practically written for the MEconomy. I'm sure you've heard this notion before, of making sure you're in the right tribe. Either you're born into a tight-knit community, and you add to it, or you create your own. In Greece, they nurture tight-knit communities, and socializing time is key. In Okinawa, groups build Moai tribes of five friends who commit to each other for life; some of these groups are more than 90 years old.

These communities and groups take us right back to the idea that who you hang out with influences who you are. The Framingham Studies brought this to national and international prevalence - smoking, happiness, obesity, loneliness, and depression are contagious. Take a look at who you hang out with now. Spend time with the right friends, and you'll be happier and healthier and way more successful.

Faith - If you are part of a regularly practicing faith community, then you know what I'm about to say here. The sense of fellowship, nurturing our purpose, and a strong belief

Go to MarkEvansDM.com/MEconomy for the chapter my publisher didn't want in the book.

and morals system can add many years to our lives - studies say between four and 14 years.

If you're not interested in organized religion, that's not necessary. Find a strong, moral-centered group that positively affects the overall community - one where the generosity of spirit and giving back is a priority. Many of us can lend a hand and give a hand up to those who are in need. Being a part of that type of community is extremely fulfilling and powerful.

Focusing on Your Loved Ones - In the MEconomy, as in the Blue Zones, we focus on our families first. We take care of our aging parents and grandparents. We are in positive, loving, and committed relationships. We care for our children and invest time and love to make sure they know how important they are to us. We build a culture of love and caring for each other.

We have to be true to our word to our family and loved ones. Good or bad. The other day, my five-year-old son was misbehaving and, frankly, being a brat. While he was running around, he spilled paint on the floor from not being careful. I told him that he was going to get a spanking on his bare bottom. He cried, and to be honest with you; I was crying after the spanking too. I don't like spanking my kids. But, I had told

Go to MarkEvansDM.com/MEconomy for the chapter my publisher didn't want in the book.

him what was going to happen, and he didn't listen, so I had to follow through so he would learn that there were consequences to his actions.

A few minutes later, I was feeling terrible, and I wanted to check in on him. He was sleeping like a baby. He was ok, and knew that I would follow through on what I said, just like if I promise him an ice cream cone, he gets an ice cream cone.

What You Can Control

You can control more about your health than you think you can. If you have put yourself into the trap that you'll have diabetes or cancer because it runs in the family, then you need to shake yourself out of that.

Years ago, I went to a doctor who ran my blood work. They didn't tell me not to eat or drink before the test, so I ate and drank before the test, and it messed things up. A few days later, I went back and was told, "Yeah, everything looks good - you're in the average of everyone else." But, I don't want to be average - I want to be optimal. Average stats are the average between the fit person and the overweight 500 lb. guy. What's optimal - that's where we need to go with our health.

That doctor, and many doctors, will tell you you're ok, but is it true? Are they just talking about the idea of being

Go to MarkEvansDM.com/MEconomy for the chapter my publisher didn't want in the book.

healthy is a lack of disease? Just because you don't officially have diabetes doesn't mean you're healthy until that moment. We've never been taught to question authority, and we often see doctors as the **only** authority on health. Unless your doctor helps you understand and achieve optimal health, you need to question your test results if they say, "Oh, everything is ok here."

On the side of mental health, we often think that we can't help how we feel about something - like feelings are something wild that we have no control over. But this just isn't true. Feelings come from our thoughts, and we can control our thoughts. Sometimes it's hard to do that, but it can be done. You can train your brain to control your thoughts. If you're thinking positive things, your brain finds it easier to think that way. If you're constantly thinking negatively, your brain finds it easier to go down that road.

Unless you can get your thought patterns positive, you can't plan and build and maintain your MEconomy. Instead, you'll be in a mental hangover state - you'll wake up feeling like crap, you can't do anything productive, you snap at people you love. You can control that state. Just like a physical hangover - you can stop drinking or leave the party earlier - you have 100% control over that. You have that same control over what your inner dialogue is telling you about you and your life.

Go to MarkEvansDM.com/MEconomy for the chapter my publisher didn't want in the book.

We have to take responsibility for our actions and words AND thoughts. The MEconomy demands it. Once you own your actions, you'll own the consequences of those actions. The same is true with your words and thoughts. It's a spiral - it's either upward or downward. Once you start on a downward spiral, it's really hard to stop and turn that around. It's much easier to stay on an upward spiral and keep climbing. Don't get pulled down by your past. Your past isn't the mirror of your FUTURE. As long as you take control over every facet of your life (today and beyond), you can control your destiny. You can't control the past, but you can control the future. Focusing only on what can be controlled is how you master the MEconomy.

Chapter 4

Daily Habits for Success

I'm not going to sit here and tell you what daily habits you need to be successful. Everyone is different - it really just takes awareness and knowing what works best for you. With that said, there are some habits that you might want to institute, especially if you feel like you're failing a little bit. Habits really can improve your mental and physical health, as well as contribute to helping you become the best you can be. In fact, I would go so far as to say that success-building daily habits are the key to creating a happy and productive MEconomy.

What works for me may not work for you. At the same time, some of the things I do daily, you might find useful. I bet

Go to MarkEvansDM.com/MEconomy for the chapter my publisher didn't want in the book.

you do something every day that I would find useful. No matter what they are, these daily habits are beneficial, as long as they contribute to your MEconomy. That is, they serve you - they improve you - they strengthen and protect you. Just like there are commonalities between people who live a long time, as we discussed in the previous chapter, there are things that successful people have in common.

Our daily goal is to be better today than we were yesterday. If you're not keeping score, KPIs if you will (Key Performance Indicators) on the quality of your life and the health of your MEconomy, you're in trouble. Let's take a look at some ideas for daily habits that successful people have in common. Some of these you'll notice are also shared by healthy, long-lived people. Coincidence?

Waking Up Early

This morning, I got up around 4:00 a.m., I grabbed my notebook and pen (I'm a little old school) and sat in silence for a bit. After a few minutes, I start thinking about my day, including how things went yesterday. I jot down some things I want to accomplish and reflect on what I need to do to improve – how can I do things better. It's a nice moment, and I use it to get my head around the day in a relaxing manner.

Go to MarkEvansDM.com/MEconomy for the chapter my publisher didn't want in the book.

The more time you make in your day to focus on being successful and building your MEconomy, the more likely you'll achieve your goals. This habit of focusing on success is a habit we see in many successful people, although there are exceptions (for any of these habits, I'm sure). Richard Branson wakes up at 5 a.m., exercises first thing, has breakfast, spends time with his family, and then gets to work. "The reason I like to wake up early is so that I can work through my emails before most of the world logs on," he explains.

Early morning hours can be very productive hours. It's quiet. Often, others in your household are still sleeping. When you wake up and get started before the day begins for most people, that one hour of productivity has an incredibly high net value. Since it's quiet, and you're most often alone, you can focus on the task at hand - and be self-aware as you start your day.

How to get an extra 30 days per year...

If you wake up 2 hours earlier everyday, multiply 365 days by 2 hours and then divide by 24 (hours in a day), you would gain another 30 FULL Days in your life. Maybe go to bed an hour later, get up an hour earlier, however the equation works best for you. Work on this one habit and you'll gain time. It's not always easy but trust me it gets easier more you do it.

I'm on this journey with you so be sure to get daily **Wakie Wakie 444** from me in your inbox.

Sign up at: *MarkEvansDM.com/444*

Go to MarkEvansDM.com/MEconomy for the chapter my publisher didn't want in the book.

Get Organized

I know there's wishful thinking about how clutter and disorganization is the sign of a genius mind, but I do think that's a bit of a myth, and there's no evidence that it's a pattern for successful people. On the contrary, when you're disorganized, whether in your workspace or even in your mind, time is wasted. There's little to no efficiency when you're spending time looking for things or floundering about with no organization in your daily work habits.

For instance, spending time checking emails throughout the day or responding to messages right away will distract you from the task at hand. Maintaining an organized work environment is one of the most commonly mentioned habits when it comes to successful individuals - and it not only includes physical organization but also setting priorities and planning.

Jack Dorsey, the co-founder, and CEO of Twitter, uses Sunday to plan and organize for the rest of the week. I use my morning time to get my planning and prioritizing done, and then set aside a time during the week to reflect on how to organize my time accordingly. Organization skills are learned behaviors. Thinking or saying that organization does not come naturally to you is no excuse. There are no excuses in the MEconomy. You can develop the discipline and focus needed

Go to MarkEvansDM.com/MEconomy for the chapter my publisher didn't want in the book.

to become organized. There are apps to help you manage and prioritize your time, and other technology can help you build good organizational habits. My go-to is pen and paper. I know there are many amazing and efficient tools we have access to, yet so many seem inefficient. Why is that? Because for me, they tend to complicate the process. The bottom line is that you need to make organization a priority habit of succeeding no matter how you get there.

Taking Action

You can plan and prioritize all you want, but those things are just potential if you don't take action on those plans and priorities. You're not truly on the road to success if you're waiting for things to happen that may or may not benefit you. It's like spending tens of thousands of dollars on an advanced degree but not building a network (more on that later) so that you can get a killer position or use that network to build your own empire.

Successful people act - they put their ideas into action. They often act before they are ready. Too often, we get paralyzed, waiting for the perfect moment, the perfect content for our website, or the perfect process for shipping our product. But that's actually counterproductive. It's always better to just put out version 1.0 - you can still fine-tune things

Go to MarkEvansDM.com/MEconomy for the chapter my publisher didn't want in the book.

later on. Like apps have Beta versions – after all, isn't life a beta - successful people take that first step, even if it seems premature. Author and entrepreneur, James Clear, talks about how successful people start before they feel ready.

Relaxation/Downtime

We talked about this in the last chapter, so we'll just touch on it here. But, I think it's important to note that relaxing, whether you're actively meditating or just trying to avoid negativity in thought, is another commonly mentioned habit of successful people. When your thoughts are organized, this becomes easier and more beneficial. Indeed, just taking a breath once in a while can help you refocus and reset your brain. By just focusing on your breathing for a few minutes, you can achieve a deep sense of relaxation that can reverse the stress response. Try it a few times a day.

For me, this is my cigar time. I might only take four or five puffs off a cigar, sit with myself, take some deep breaths, and focus on my thoughts and actions. Meditation and downtime are different for everyone -- it can be a focused, structured meditation or a relaxing gathering with friends. It doesn't matter. It's about whatever works best for you and balances your life out.

Go to MarkEvansDM.com/MEconomy for the chapter my publisher didn't want in the book.

Staying Positive

Most of the successful entrepreneurs I've met and have worked with are natural optimists. You have to be to go into business for yourself - especially since so many new businesses fail. But that optimism keeps them going until they find the right business, the right formula, that finally means success for them. But this state of mind is not just for entrepreneurs. A positive viewpoint is one of the main ingredients to success, not just being successful like most people think.

Joel Brown specializes in this area and in helping entrepreneurs tap into success. Being grateful and positive is a priority for building your MEconomy. Brown talks about how it's not good enough just to express gratitude about your life; you have to look at why you're grateful. I think this goes back to knowing your purpose and why you wake up each morning. That can help you focus on staying positive, focused, organized, and grateful.

Go to MarkEvansDM.com/MEconomy for the chapter my publisher didn't want in the book.

Taking Care of Yourself

Taking care of yourself is about mental and physical health, as well as emotional and spiritual health. Health is not an accident. It takes work, but once you're in a good state of mind, body, and spirit, it's easier to maintain. In addition to what we've talked about in the last chapter, this also includes daily hygiene. Elon Musk, CEO of Tesla Motors and SpaceX, put it this way when asked what daily habit he felt was critical to success. In true Elon Musk style, he answered quickly, "Showering."

Spending Wisely

Smart and successful people don't overspend, and they certainly don't spend beyond their means. Want to be successful? Analyze each purchase you make carefully - it's going to serve you and your MEconomy well, or it's going to deplete resources. There are very rarely "neutral" financial decisions you can make. The bottom line for spending money, and being smart with your money, is to spend it only on things you need or things that advance your MEconomy.

You can include things you want, but for things that help you live out your image of success in a smart way - in other words, the benefits outweigh the expenditure. As I see

Go to MarkEvansDM.com/MEconomy for the chapter my publisher didn't want in the book.

it, people's biggest problem is that they try to save themselves to wealth when what they need to be doing is to exhaust their brain space on how to earn more. Keep in mind that when you are successful, and by all accounts, rich, you don't have to throw your money around. Billionaire Warren Buffet lives in the same house he bought back in 1958, in Omaha, Nebraska, for under $32,000.

Network, network, network!

To be a success, it is really about who you know. If you only know a few people, your chances will be few. If you know many people and have meaningful relationships with them, your opportunities to succeed grow exponentially. You have to be willing to share your time and collaborate with others who are also pursuing success. In the previous chapter, we talked about surrounding yourself with people you want to be like and building your tribe. Networking is about taking that same concept into a business setting. To be successful, you surround yourself with other successful people. You learn from them, and they learn from you.

Thomas Corley nails this, I think. The author of "Rich Habits: The Daily Success Habits of Wealthy Individuals," Corley studied over 150 self-made millionaires for over five years. He learned that rich people deliberately surround

Go to MarkEvansDM.com/MEconomy for the chapter my publisher didn't want in the book.

themselves with rich people. It's powerful to know a lot of great people. But massive wealth comes from who knows YOU. Think about Michael Jordan and how much money he makes because he's so well-known. He knows the right people, and the masses know him!

Almost 80% of wealthy individuals spend, at a minimum, five hours each month networking. When I talk about networking, it isn't just about going to a networking event. You could be meeting business people at dinner and talking about business plans and objectives, how you're going to reach goals, and other related topics. Networking should be a habit whenever you are with other business people.

Give Back

One hundred percent of the profits from this book will be donated to charity. You are indirectly giving to charity and learning as well. In my world, we call this Full Circle Giving. I am sharing my time and knowledge, you spend a few dollars to learn, and that money gets donated to a charity that will better the lives of people we will never meet.

The most successful people give back to their community. They know that their success, in many ways, is on the back of others, and they believe in the value of sharing and giving back.

Go to MarkEvansDM.com/MEconomy for the chapter my publisher didn't want in the book.

I was recently at a charity dinner, where Superbowl tickets came up for bid. I won the auction and was so psyched to go. But, a few days later, I turned to my wife and said, "You know, what if we gave those tickets to someone who wouldn't be able to go to a game like this?" From there, we held a contest and met a beautiful young man with terminal cancer.

We paid for his and his family's first-class airfare, hotel, and all other travel arrangements. We went as well - and the next day after the game, I checked in with him at the hotel. We both cried, feeling so grateful. He now gives what time he has left giving back, too - via a podcast where he shares stories of hope and survival. As long as this young boy is around and beyond, I know the true nature of giving back and how much it gives to me emotionally and spiritually.

The accumulation of wealth, in and of itself, is a selfish act. So, to be truly successful, you have to look beyond that accumulation and look for ways to benefit others. Warren Buffet is an exemplary example of sharing and giving back. He is extremely generous with his wealth, investing in programs that do work for the greater good. He turned 90 on August 30, 2020, and as of that date, had given $37 billion to charity.

You're not off the hook if you're not wealthy — yet. If you don't have millions to start your own foundation, you can donate whenever and wherever you can. In Covid times, $50

Go to MarkEvansDM.com/MEconomy for the chapter my publisher didn't want in the book.

to contribute to a local food bank can make a big difference. You can also donate time and services, whether you're wealthy or not. That type of service doesn't cost you anything and can bring great benefit to your community. Help where and when you can, however, you can. Think of giving to those in need like a muscle. You have to work out and exercise it so it becomes natural for you to give.

Giving can also mean something more personal - sometimes I sit in the quiet part of the morning and write a letter to those I care about - my mom, my wife. I regularly buy coffee for the people behind me in the drive-through.

Giving back is also being present for those around you. If we're caught up all day in the details of making money, of being successful, we can leave people behind. By giving back, we're making an incredible connection with others. Even strangers, some of whom become friends.

There are many ways to give back but rest assured, it's a muscle that one must know exists and constantly put pressure on to grow.

Read (and Learn)

J.K. Rowling, best-selling author of the Harry Potter series, can help us think about how important reading and learning is. She says, "Read as much as you possibly can.

75

Nothing will help you as much..." Most successful people read for pleasure, and they also tap into their habit of reading to gain knowledge and insight into their world. Tom Corley would add, "Reading every day to learn is one of the most powerful happiness activities we can engage in...unsuccessful people are not students of their industry, profession or trade."

That seems like a pretty good trade-off. Take a few minutes or an hour each day to read something - whether it's for pleasure or learning, the payoff is huge. If you can't find time to read, listen to educational podcasts or audiobooks. I'm not talking about Gone With the Wind here. I'm talking about non-fiction books that increase your knowledge— books on marketing, finance, and self-help. We need to continuously knowledge up. There are no excuses in the MEconomy

Fun fact - I've read over 5,000 books. What's even more interesting is that I never read a book until I was out of high school. It's true! The first book I ever read was Think and Grow Rich by Napoleon Hill - which I recommend we ALL read once a year. Another fact - I'm the slowest reader under the sun. It takes me a long time to read and to retain the information. But the outcome is well worth the effort.

Get a list of my top 100 books.
Go to: *MarkEvansDM.com/top100*

Go to MarkEvansDM.com/MEconomy for the chapter my publisher didn't want in the book.

The Bottom Line

Most people have habits - but are they good or bad? If you're human and like me, you probably have both types of habits. Unsuccessful people have a lot of bad habits. But habits are changeable. Successful people have habits that create success, and they also know that they can always improve themselves and become more successful.

To this day, I am still asked about when I'm going to stop dreaming and get a real job? Well then, answer me this. What does that even mean? If it means I have to do something I don't want to do, or work hard for someone else, no thanks. If it means I have to beg for a day off to get to watch, my kids play a sport...um...no.

NEVER STOP LEARNING... just because you're out of high school or college doesn't mean you are done learning. The truth is you're just starting. You must constantly be learning and realize you don't know much on the grand schemes of things. Invest in yourself via mentoring programs, coaches, online courses for your finances, health, relationships etc.

When I think of success in my life, I think of how my businesses feed my family life. So I pay attention to my businesses and who I work with because it is an extension of me. Now, I can't control every aspect or outcome of the

Go to MarkEvansDM.com/MEconomy for the chapter my publisher didn't want in the book.

business, but I can control things like the business's culture, how the team works with each other and with each other. I can learn to let go of things that others can do better.

I can't worry about spending $100 to make $1,000. Short-sighted thinking never works - really, not even for the short-term. When I choose to focus on the people living successfully, and that means happy and healthy, as well as any wealth they have, I know I'm looking in the right direction.

Think of a football team and how every player has a specific role. In life, to be successful and develop appropriate success-generating habits, we have to determine our role on our team. The team can be in our family, in our community, at work - it doesn't matter. The team happens together, and when we balance things in our life.

Achieving success is not done in a straight line. You have to be looking all around you, all the time. And balance your life between work, family, and self-care. You can only achieve this by developing and nurturing good habits - healthy habits - and productive habits. If not, any security you think you might have in your bubble is just a lie. Your habits are the only way to reinforce your bubble, creating a true MEconomy protected from uncertainty and outside forces.

Fall in love with the journey - you do that by developing these good habits. You're stacking up wins instead of losses. If you maintain good habits, you're winning. Likewise, if you're

Go to MarkEvansDM.com/MEconomy for the chapter my publisher didn't want in the book.

perpetuating bad habits, you're losing. There will be days you don't feel like reading; read anyway. There will be days you're too tired to eat well; do it anyway. The more wins you have, the more success you'll have. You'll also be happier and healthier, two great byproducts of these good habits.

It's easy when it's easy. The magic is in when it's not easy, and you do it anyway. Follow the North Star. That's what will drive you and help you get up every day.

DM RECOMMENDATION

If you are struggling with how to start winning and getting back on track mentally and physically, YOU must get on this program today. It's FREE by the way (so can't use money as an excuse).

75 Hard was put together by Andy Frisella. It will get you on track and realize how powerful YOU really are as person. If you're overweight this is a must! If you're scattered and unfocused in life, this is a must! If you are anxious and overwhelmed with life, this is a must! If you want help but not sure where to start, this is the starting point!

Go to: **75Hard.com**

Go to MarkEvansDM.com/MEconomy for the chapter my publisher didn't want in the book.

Chapter 5

Change the Script

We lie to ourselves all day long. We convince ourselves that we can or can't do something. That's a classic way to live in someone else's economy. When we neglect our responsibilities to own our actions, we're lying to everyone around us, but mostly to ourselves. To make stratospheric changes, you have to stop the lie; you have to shift the script.

This includes what you tell yourself and others. We say things to ourselves that we would never say to a loved one. We call ourselves names and belittle our efforts all the time. We've been trained to self-evaluate and criticize. It wreaks havoc on what we can accomplish, the quality of our social circle, and extremely limits our ability to succeed in life.

We learn these patterns from our parents, siblings, and family members. We also learn it in the schools. So, the way

Go to MarkEvansDM.com/MEconomy for the chapter my publisher didn't want in the book.

you can break those negative patterns and develop more positive thinking is to educate yourself. Once again, you have more control here than you think. You can 100% control what goes in your head, your thoughts, and what comes out of your mouth. Don't believe me? Let's look at the science behind this.

Neuroplasticity

The plasticity of the brain, or its ability to adapt and change, is a recent discovery. Back in the day, we pretty much thought that your brain could only decline. Researchers believed that the only time your brain could change was during infancy and early childhood. By the time you were an adult, the belief had gone, your brain's structure was pretty permanent. But, now we know that our brain is malleable. It can learn to do things differently.

In the early part of the 20th century, we discovered neural pathways; these are the routes that electrical signals take in your brain. By the 60s, scientists started looking at older adults who had experienced massive strokes and how they could relearn functions once thought to be triggered in specific areas of the brain. So, the beginnings of this plasticity of the brain started to take shape.

Go to MarkEvansDM.com/MEconomy for the chapter my publisher didn't want in the book.

Now we know that the brain is continuously adapting neural pathways and creating new ones to react to new realities. In other words, we're not just stuck with the brain we have - we can improve our brain's efficiency and create new neural pathways. But what does this have to do with changing your script? Even though the average neuron of a three-year-old has about 15,000 synapses, by the time you're an adult, you have about half that number?

That's the plasticity right there. We're not functioning half as well; we're getting more efficient. Some connections are getting stronger, and others not used as often are dying as the brain learns what works and what doesn't. This brain activity is known as pruning.

But, let's get out of the brain for a second and bring this back to earth.

The Path Less Taken

I want you to think of a hiking path. You know how a well-traveled path becomes very wide and smooth - it's easy to find your way. If you've ever been hiking, you know that sometimes you take a wrong turn, and suddenly the path starts to get more overgrown, and you are having a hard time finding your way.

Go to MarkEvansDM.com/MEconomy for the chapter my publisher didn't want in the book.

Your neural pathways are just like this. If you are constantly thinking negatively, you are building a hiking path for the neural electrical charges to travel down. The more you think negatively, the wider and easier to navigate that pathway becomes. If you start thinking positively, you're creating a new path, and it's not as wide or smooth, so it's tough to stay positive at first.

The more you travel that positivity pathway, the easier and easier it becomes to stay on that path. And guess what? As you are now traveling on that positive path, those negative neural pathways become overgrown and harder to navigate. So your brain has rewired itself to think positively. It has pruned the pathways that don't serve you any longer, and your attitude in life has taken a major shift.

Easier said than done. You literally have to retrain your brain. Just like the person who has suffered a stroke needs to build new pathways for speech or walking. You have to put yourself through a similar type of training program, and there are no shortcuts. You can't just wake up one day with new, more constructive, and positive paths in your brain. You have to start to break down the destructive pathways that no longer serve you, and at the same time, lay down some new pathways.

The good news is that this plasticity in your brain is ongoing. If you're reading this book, your brain still has its

Go to MarkEvansDM.com/MEconomy for the chapter my publisher didn't want in the book.

plasticity. As we age, it might take a little longer to achieve new pathways for new thoughts and outlooks, but it's certainly possible. Once we can identify which pathways we need to build and which we need to break down, it's a little bit easier. Start journaling daily on gratitude to open up new paths and to see new paths. I'm grateful I can read, I can see, I have a heartbeat. What are you grateful for?

Know Thyself

Scientists have identified several types of cognitive distortions that we can rewire. I won't get into all of them because I'm not a brain expert. But I do want to highlight a few. See if you recognize some of these in yourself. Keep in mind, MEconomy demands that you're honest with yourself. Any of these seem familiar?

- *Black and white thinking.* Thinking in either/or instead of seeing the whole situation.
- *Catastrophizing.* Making a mountain out of a molehill. Taking something trivial and making it a tragedy.
- *Filtering.* This is your classic negative thought when you filter out any positives and only look at the negatives.

- *Overgeneralization.* Just because something bad happened once in a certain scenario, it will always be that way. Or thinking that one bad thing, like bombing on a test, means you'll probably fail the class.
- *Victim syndrome.* Thinking that external factors are to blame for your woes.
- *Worrying about others too much.* Of course, we want to care for others, but if you think you said or did something that made someone else do x, y, z, that's destructive. This sounds like, "Did I say something that hurt you?" Of course, be sensitive to other peoples' feelings, but don't internalize that.
- *Taking everything personally.* When you feel that someone did something just to hurt you, the truth is, most of the time, no one is thinking about or worried about you when making decisions about their own life. Chill out!
- *Jumping to conclusions.* See taking everything personally and filtering. Find out and consider all the facts and perspectives. Be wise. Not quick to jump.
- *Blame game.* Blaming yourself for everything that goes wrong or blaming others for your pain. doesn't mean you shouldn't take responsibility, but that's very different than attaching blame.

- *Emperor syndrome.* Thinking that you're always right - you'll argue with people who think that maybe you aren't right. This is a great way to push people away from you and make tons of mistakes. You're not always right. No one is.

Seriously look at the above list. Take an honest inventory of your present and past. We all tap into these occasionally, but if you're stuck in these patterns, you're destroying your ability to build a MEconomy, and you're greatly limiting your power and legacy. Great leaders have fallen victim to these patterns, tarnishing their reputation and sometimes taking down their admirers with them.

When you can see who you are, you can honestly rise above any of these negative ways of thinking and conquer just about anything. So the good news is that you most certainly can shatter these terrible thinking habits and create new, much more pleasant, and productive neural pathways in your brain.

Here's how.

How to Retrain Your Brain

Think of this as a basic toolkit - like I've said before, what works for me doesn't necessarily work for you and vice versa. The thing to remember is that it takes time and practice to make these shifts in your brain. I mean, think about it, you've had decades of negative thought pathways, probably. It will take a while to let that path overgrow. But, you'll be surprised how quickly that can happen if you practice, every day, in little and big ways, to change your narrative.

Pay Attention to Your Thoughts

Just like you have to admit you have a problem before making a major life change, like quitting drinking or drugs - you have to know yourself and what your thinking errors are before you can change them. So the first thing you need to do is take stock of that. Once you've identified your negative patterns, you can detach from them.

There are a variety of ways you can tackle this. Some people find it useful to keep a journal and jot down negative thoughts as they happen. At the end of the day, you can look at that and see what patterns emerge. Do you tend toward filtering or emperor syndrome? In what circumstances, or around which people you tend to have negative thoughts and ideas. Pay special attention to your self-talk. What are you saying about YOU to yourself? Jot down any negative thoughts you have. Jot down ALL your thoughts. This is called *Thought Auditing.*

Go to **MarkEvansDM.com/MEconomy** for the chapter my publisher didn't want in the book.

> *"You cannot win the war against the world if you cannot win the war against your own mind. Self-discipline is the center of all material success."*
> **Daniel Nwaelel, Jr**

Another way to take control of negative thoughts is through a type of meditation. Pick a time every day that you can commit to sitting still in your thoughts for a few minutes. This meditation is more mindful than the type we talked about to wind down. Here you're focusing on your breath, yes, but you're also paying close attention to what your thoughts are. You're not dwelling on them - you're letting them come into your brain and then right out. Just say "hi," and let them go. At the end of the meditation, jot down what you learned, and make it a point to think more positively about whatever popped into your head during the meditation.

This type of awareness has a couple of advantages. First, again, it lets you take inventory of where you're at with your thoughts, so you can start reverse-thinking the negative ideas that come into your brain. Mindfulness also helps with reducing your stress levels and making you a little less reactionary.

Go to MarkEvansDM.com/MEconomy for the chapter my publisher didn't want in the book.

Trigger (un)Happy

When we're completely honest with ourselves, one of the things we understand about our personality is what sets us off. What are our triggers? We hate to think that something outside of us has control over our reaction - that goes against the MEconomy for sure - but knowing that there might be particular places, things, and people that trigger you in a negative way is the first stop of putting those to rest.

Do you have a relative that just gets under your skin? There's a trigger. Do you get really anxious when you're about to give a presentation? Trigger. What about a colleague or client that you don't quite see eye-to-eye? Trigger!

But don't blame those people or situations. It's on you, and you have to identify those triggers and then neutralize them. Most of the time, your easiest route will be to change up the situation. If you're prepping for a presentation, listen to some calming music, or something that will pump you up. Or smoke a cigar—something to change how you usually prepare and something that gets you feeling a little more comfortable.

If it's a person that triggers you, you have a couple of choices. First, you could avoid the person. That doesn't fix anything, but if it's someone you really don't need in your life, let them go. If you can't avoid someone in your life - like

89

Go to MarkEvansDM.com/MEconomy for the chapter my publisher didn't want in the book.

maybe a colleague or relative, you have to adapt how you think about things to neutralize any negative reaction that you might have. If you feel your face burning, take a (not literal) step back as you get more stressed. Take a couple of deep breaths, and push any negative thoughts in a different direction. A trick that works great is to change the subject. It's critical to remember that you CAN'T change anyone. You have to change yourself and how you approach toxic people in your life. Don't give in to their behavior, and don't let them get to you. Your boundaries, your MEconomy, must be protected. I don't care who they are, or what they've meant to you in the past. Toxic people have no place in the MEconomy.

Negative to Positive

We ALL have negative thoughts. But the difference is how we act on them and how much we let them affect us. Once we get into that negative spiral, we build that pathway again if we don't change it. Instead, we have to stop and recognize the negative thought and counter it with a positive thought. This positive thinking greatly improves our well-being. Research has also shown that it can decrease feelings of depression and general sadness.

Remember Droopy the Dog or Eeyore? We sound just like them when we get into this type of negative thinking. "It

Go to MarkEvansDM.com/MEconomy for the chapter my publisher didn't want in the book.

will never work..." First of all, anyone you want in your life isn't going to want to be around someone negative. So, all of these tips will help you find and keep amazing people in your life. Second, these negative thoughts do not serve you!

Instead, challenge yourself. Is what you said true? Does it serve you? Change your focus and outlook. Sure, maybe something isn't happening the way you planned, so you're frustrated. Acknowledge that, and figure out how to move forward from your new reality. Focus on creating solutions NOT the problem.

I love the "Name it to Tame It" method by Dr. Daniel Siegel. Here we look our negative thoughts right in the face and name them. Have fun with this to change your mood, too. If you find yourself, for instance, blaming yourself or others all the time, you can call yourself on it. "Ah, there's that Blame Game," or "Here comes the emperor." This can be helpful after taking inventory of your negative thoughts and knowing your patterns well. Make fun of yourself, but in a loving way.

Attitude of Gratitude

We talked about this already, but just as practicing gratitude can help you with your stress levels, it can also help you shift your negative to positive thoughts. We have a lot to be grateful about - but if we've been walking that negative path for too long, it can be hard to see the forest through the trees - we can lose sight of the good things we have in life.

Repeat After Me

I'm sure you've heard of affirmations and mantras. These are things you say to yourself to help you shift your focus from negative to positive. They may sound kind of hokey, but they work. The more we repeat something to ourselves, the more real it feels and becomes. This is part of the practice it takes to wear out old negative paths and build some new, positive pathways in your brain.

Most of the time, when we're thinking negatively, we're talking ourselves out of something. We're giving in to our fear or feelings of inadequacy. Again, if you've taken inventory of your negative thoughts, you'll know which ones you need to address. If you're constantly calling yourself stupid or lazy, your mantra or affirmation needs to address it directly. As soon as you hear yourself putting yourself down, you counter with just the opposite. "I'm stupid," becomes "I'm smart, and I'm always learning." "I'm lazy," becomes "I'm active and moving."

These aren't denying reality. If you are lazy, by saying to yourself that you're active and moving, you're more likely to get off your butt and move. So mantras can motivate you and inspire you. The key is to make a major shift in your thinking. Because these mantras might feel a little weird and silly at first, I'm here to tell you that the more awkward it feels, it probably means that it's exactly what you need to be telling yourself. I want to be clear. It's not just enough to say, but to actually start doing is where the results start showing up.

When you're feeling anxious and stressed, say to yourself, "Yeah, I got this." If you're feeling less-than, tell yourself that "I am worth it." If you're feeling depressed or pissed, "I choose to be grateful and calm." If you're my age, you'll probably remember the Saturday Night Live character, Stuart Smalley, of "I'm good enough, I'm smart enough and doggone it, people like me." It was a funny joke because there's a small amount of truth to it, I know. But, trust me, they can really work to build new pathways.

Morning Routines

I want to mention morning routines specific to positive thinking. A good morning routine gets your day started on the right foot. Develop whatever routine works for you, and make sure it includes enough sleep the night before, hydration, a good meal, movement, and some time for quiet and reflection.

Go to MarkEvansDM.com/MEconomy for the chapter my publisher didn't want in the book.

My Morning Routine:

I control when I get up! I may not like it very often but my internal clock has me up on or before 4:44 am 7 days a week. Of course, this isn't 100%, but it's almost daily.

Get up early. This starts the day with a Win.

Journal Session. Take 15 minutes to go over the day and what your grateful for.

Plan for a successful day. Most don't have a plan but to make it to the end of the day. (Don't be that person)

Drink water. Sounds silly but get the fluids rolling asap.

Food prep for the day. Health requires preparation.

Check your money flow. Many don't know where they are financially. Know where your money is at all times.

Input. Listen to a positive book, podcast show and or pull out the good ole book and read and knowledge up.

Exercise. I like to get this in earlier the better be done by 8 am or earlier. Something is better than nothing.

See you can get a lot done before most of the world even gets out of bed! Brag about getting up early to accomplish your dreams. Don't brag about how you sleep in late everyday.

Go to MarkEvansDM.com/MEconomy for the chapter my publisher didn't want in the book.

Pay it Forward

Nothing gets you out of a funk better than helping someone else out. Famous early 20th-century psychiatrist Alfred Adler put it best, *"You can be healed of depression if every day you begin the first thing in the morning to consider how you will bring real joy to someone else."*

Basically, by helping others, we avoid depression, and we feel like we're making a difference. Most people donate to causes they believe in because it makes them feel good. Acts of kindness make you happy. Making someone else have a better day helps you forget about whatever might be dragging you down.

These don't have to be huge gestures. Keep your life simple. Pay for a stranger's toll or support a local starving artist. Participate in neighborhood cleanup activities. Donate to someone's charity drive. Call a friend you haven't talked to in a while. Write someone a text to let them know you're thinking about them. Do something like this every day, and you'll soon find that your negative thinking replaced with a more positive outlook.

Here is a 30-day challenge for you. When you're in drive-through getting coffee, pay for the stranger behind you. No questions asked. Do this for 30 days, and before you know it, it's a normal thing you do. Or, if you're at a coffee shop, pay

Go to MarkEvansDM.com/MEconomy for the chapter my publisher didn't want in the book.

for the person behind you. Remember, YOU can't outgive the world.

Change Your Environment

Change your view. Sometimes our thought patterns are based on the world around us. If you find yourself feeling negatively in a certain setting, change your view. Go for a walk or a drive in the country. Get out of Dodge for a weekend. Whenever you can, spend some time in nature - there's no better way to relieve some stress and anxiety.

Most importantly, make sure your environment includes positive people. Turn to them when you need a lift. If you are in a place where no one is positive, hop online and join a mastermind group or free Facebook group where people are positive and not judging you for the old you but inspire you to become a better YOU!

Change the Script, Change Your Life

In the MEconomy, you are taking total responsibility for your internal script. If it's negative, you need to throw it out. You can change your script by taking it by the horns, knowing what you're dealing with, identifying your negative thoughts and patterns around them, and then flipping that script. Walk a

Go to MarkEvansDM.com/MEconomy for the chapter my publisher didn't want in the book.

different pathway, and let the old, tired, negative path grow over with weeds. You've got more important trails to blaze.

Chapter 6

The Myth of Education

My wife and I homeschool our kids - and we always knew we would. Most of the time, when we tell people we're homeschooling, their eyes pop open, and they look at us like we're crazy, asking us, "When are your kids going to get the chance to socialize?" or "How are they going to learn from their peers?" I always roll my eyes, or at least I imagine I do, and think, "Yeah, so your kids are going to socialize sitting in class and told to sit down and be quiet all day?"

We know the school system is broken, but I'm sure that most people also think that to some degree or another. But when most Americans say the school system is broken, I think they're thinking about test scores, college admissions, and SAT scores. Our take is a little different. We don't worry about grades, test scores, or even college admissions. We

Go to MarkEvansDM.com/MEconomy for the chapter my publisher didn't want in the book.

want our kids to be happy, high-functioning adults with common sense, critical thinking, and problem-solving skills. That's not something most schools offer.

I didn't do great in school. That might not be a great surprise to most anyone who knows me. I acted up. I was bored. I didn't get why we had to learn certain things. I even cheated, or what I like to call collaboration - shh - don't tell my parents. But, I know I'm happy, I'm healthy, contribute to society, and make a lot of money. We are prioritizing the wrong things in school.

For example, so many kids are not fluent in basic financial literacy. Now, tell me what I need to know more - how to put together a budget and spend money wisely, or which general led the attack on Gondola Hills in the war of 1812? (Don't look that up - I just made it up!)

There's a myth in this country that Education (yes, with a capital E, like it's some formal, organized system) is the great Equalizer. I call BS. The United States' education system lets a few poor kids slip through and achieve power, but it's almost an accident. It allows a few lower-middle-class kids to make it big. For the most part, this country's education system is designed to do one thing and one thing only; it's designed to keep you in your place.

Go to MarkEvansDM.com/MEconomy for the chapter my publisher didn't want in the book.

Let's take a brief (I promise) look at the history of education in the United States of America - when we can see where it came from, this will all be crystal clear.

A Brief History

When our country was first established, there was no such thing as public education. Education was reserved only for people with money - reading and writing wasn't a priority. In those days, children were to help the family on the farm and in the home. If children were lucky enough to get some education, it would have been handled by family members. Homeschooling was the system of education.

In the 1600s (don't worry, I'll speed this up), the only reason you needed to know how to read was to read the bible - and that was only for the boys. Once settlements started to grow, into the 1700s, colonies began to set up schools, but they were for the wealthy population. Formal education just wasn't considered that important, in general.

Let's move up to the 1800s. Education shifted from a focus on religious education to more public education. The first public school in America was founded in 1821. By 1870 - after the Civil War - there were public schools in every state. But a few years later, there was a terrible depression, and many of those schools closed for lack of funding.

Go to MarkEvansDM.com/MEconomy for the chapter my publisher didn't want in the book.

We bounced back, though, and by the 1920s, we were back in business - literally. When public education was reborn, the focus was to ensure children were prepared and ready to work in the factories. By now, the agricultural way of life was changing to more city-based work. So, we had to train kids to be employees versus contributing directly to the family and home. Remember, public education came out of the industrial age. Who profits from the education system?

It was the start of how today's modern educational system operates. Let's think about what it takes to be a good employee.

The Status Quo

First and foremost, you must do what you're told to do to be a good employee. You don't ask questions - you just do your job. You have to show up every day and on time, at a certain time. You don't question authority - the boss is the boss, and you are the subordinate. You're not supposed to think - you're just supposed to do. And only the way you're shown to do something.

Don't even think about talking back - you'll get punished or even fired. You're not supposed to ask "why" you're doing things a certain way - you're just supposed to do

Go to MarkEvansDM.com/MEconomy for the chapter my publisher didn't want in the book.

it. To put it bluntly, you're a paid servant - making money for someone else in the corner office.

No, the education system is not designed to be the great equalizer. The system of education is designed to make you a great employee. In most schools, you're a good student as long as you do what they tell you. You don't ask questions - you just do what the teacher tells you to do. You show up to school at a certain time, take your breaks and lunch, and get dismissed at a certain time. You don't dare question authority - the teacher is the boss, and you're the subordinate. You're not supposed to think - you're just supposed to memorize. And, you're only supposed to memorize what they tell you to memorize.

Don't you dare talk back to the teacher - you'll get punished. You're not supposed to question why you're learning what you're learning - you're just supposed to memorize it. You're an unpaid servant - so that someone in the corner office keeps you in your place.

Look at the people who have succeeded greatly in this world. Think of the old-timers like the Rockefeller's and Kennedy's. Do you think they built their fortunes by behaving" this way? Do you think they kept their fortunes by encouraging others to challenge their authority and place in society?
If you're born poor, you're most likely to die poor, and you're born lower-middle-class, you'll probably end up lower-middle-

Go to MarkEvansDM.com/MEconomy for the chapter my publisher didn't want in the book.

class your whole life. Whether you follow the rules or not, you're very unlikely to achieve financial security beyond what your parents achieved. Like I said before, some people squeak through - but it's almost by chance. There are plenty of people who work their asses off their whole lives, make good decisions, and still don't advance their socio-economic status.

That's no accident. Trust me.

How is this possible? We all have access to the same information. Have you wondered what information some our consuming while others are ignoring it? Or maybe they are being told information that isn't intended to produce freedom.

We have to ask ourselves some questions about the education system. Yes, it's failing. But, not because kids aren't getting good test scores. What the heck does that have to do with your ability to do well in life? Almost nothing! No, the questions we have to ask are those that dig a little deeper.

What are we teaching our kids, and why? What are we teaching them to be? Who profits from our system of education? Do our kids need to know the 8th-grade state standards for history when they don't even know how to reconcile their checking account? Are we teaching our kids to be independent thinkers or sheep? Are we teaching them to be leaders or followers?

We know the answers, and the answers aren't pretty. It's our job as parents (and students) to learn basic skills, yes, but then make sure that we know how to think and question. We need to know how to ask questions and find problems and most importantly, provide solutions to those problems. We need to contribute to our society in a positive way and make sure we're helping those who might need a hand. We need to be proud and productive citizens of this great country of ours.

We need to ask ourselves this: is our education system, with its overemphasis on standardized testing and learning, the best way to educate our kids? As our world changes exponentially every day, with new technologies and new demands, are we teaching our kids what they need to know? Are we teaching them leadership skills, emotional intelligence, and the thinking skills needed to overcome everyday challenges? Are educators changing their methods of teaching to keep up in this more modern world?

About 95% of our country's students attend public school. On the one hand, it's amazing that education is accessible - more than it's ever been, with more options like charter schools. But, when it comes down to it, not much has changed from those first public schools in the 1870s. Don't count on the public school system improving to any extent, any time soon.

Go to MarkEvansDM.com/MEconomy for the chapter my publisher didn't want in the book.

And this might answer the question we get asked all the time. "Why are you homeschooling your kids?" Why? Because we don't want them to be sheep. Is that what you want for your kids? Or do you want something better for them?

We are in the middle of a pandemic that has changed the way we school our kids globally. Because of this, most of us are forced to homeschool. And I believe this has put the education system in jeopardy. People are starting to wake up and realize that homeschooling isn't such a bad thing.

Many parents have seen their kids grow and thrive as a person, not a collective. Families have reconnected in ways they hadn't even realized were missing. The family unit has become stronger again.

I realize some things need to be worked out. We need to find ways to allow our kids to socialize again. Some kids are not thriving for various reasons, and we need to figure out a solution for them. But overall, I think we all know that the education system as we know it is very broken. And we need to deal with it. It requires a complete revamping and new life to serve and teach our children the right things, not just how to be servants to the corner office.

Go to MarkEvansDM.com/MEconomy for the chapter my publisher didn't want in the book.

To College or not to College - That is the Question

We have long been told that we have to have a college education to get far in life. You absolutely must have a high school diploma, of course - or, so we're told. If you did go to college, your parents broke the bank, putting you through school, or you amassed a fortune of debt in student loans.

Well, I hate to break it to you - whoever told you this lied. Ok, that might be a bit harsh. Chances are they told you in all sincerity because they didn't know better - because they had been lied to, as well.

First, let's break the myth that you need a high school diploma. Yes, I know that many jobs and trade schools require you to have a diploma or a GED. But, there's a way for high school kids who are, let's face it, too smart to be in high school. Since most community colleges allow kids, with parental permission, to attend school before they've graduated from high school, a student who is bored to tears in high school can take college-level classes.

After so many credits - usually 6-8 college-level courses does the trick - they can enroll in a university, or just continue getting a valuable two-year Associate's degree or finishing a certificate program. Once they've achieved that level, no one will ask about a high school diploma. If this sounds like an option that might work for your kids, check with

Go to MarkEvansDM.com/MEconomy for the chapter my publisher didn't want in the book.

your local community college to see if your 15 or 16-year-old can move past their peers pretty quickly.

There are plenty of reasons why you can skip a college education altogether. Of course, if your dream is to be a doctor or a CPA, you do have to jump through some hoops, including degrees, certifications, licenses, etc. But let's take a look at reality for the vast majority of us.

More than ever, in today's fast-changing society, employers are not as interested in degrees as they used to be. They're hiring based on talent and skills, as well as any connections you might have. I barely graduated from high school. I didn't go to college because, truthfully, I didn't want to go to college. I have friends who got college degrees and who have never, not once, used the information they got from their schooling.

I'm a successful entrepreneur without a college degree. For most of us, college isn't an effective way to spend your time or money to prepare you for the workforce. Especially now - most hiring managers want to know if you're dependable, have a portfolio to prove your skills, can meet deadlines, and work in a team environment. College certainly isn't needed if you're looking to be an entrepreneur. You can learn everything you need from the free university I call YouTube. And we know the real way to learn is by doing.

Go to MarkEvansDM.com/MEconomy for the chapter my publisher didn't want in the book.

College doesn't prepare you for a job - it only teaches you the theory and maybe some history and fundamentals of your chosen industry. Sure, completing a college degree shows everyone you can finish something, but isn't it more valuable and impressive to have achieved something real? Like starting a reading program for disadvantaged youth in your community or starting a nonprofit to help homeless vets?

How are people hired for positions, anyway? Usually with some kind of resume, but they're so outdated and ridiculous in today's world. First of all, most employers don't even really read the resume and certainly don't dive deep into them. If they do, they're more interested in your experience than the education portion of the resume. The only time that a college degree is needed, as I said, is if it's a job you want, and it requires a college degree. If that's the case, get your degree, but don't go into debt doing it or putting your parents in debt.

I see kids going to college to satisfy their parents all the time; and doing what the parents think they should do. Remember, it's your life, if you don't want to do what mommy and daddy think you should do that's ok you can change - OWN IT. Sure, it's going to upset and piss people off. I didn't say creating the MEconomy was going to be rainbow and unicorns.

I want to share one more thing here (as you may be a

Go to MarkEvansDM.com/MEconomy for the chapter my publisher didn't want in the book.

parent yourself): Don't be the parent that puts your shit (*the stuff you wish you would have done or went to school for*) on your kids. We're in different times and they aren't you. I talk to a lot of parents that have their kids path mapped out for them before they are 5. At the end of the day, don't we want our kids to do better than us and be genuinely happy?

I know, I know what you're saying, "Mark, you're not realistic. It's really hard to make it without a college degree." Yeah, maybe. But, guess what? Life is really hard sometimes. It's not that you're automatically going to be successful if you don't have a college degree - it's just that I don't think you need one for most successful careers. There are plenty of people who didn't waste their time or money on a college degree. Here are just a few:

Richard Branson
Rachael Ray
Steven Spielberg
Michael Dell
Steve Jobs
Me

These aren't the only folks who have found great success without a college degree. In 2015, about one in three

Go to MarkEvansDM.com/MEconomy for the chapter my
publisher didn't want in the book.

billionaires didn't have a college degree. The percentage of billionaires with at least a Bachelor's degree continues to fall.

The truth is there are great-paying jobs and careers out there that don't require a degree at all. Not even an Associate's degree or certificate. A plumber might have to go to a trade school, for example. It's a good-paying job with lots of independence, way more than the average desk job. Other trades like mechanics, carpenters, and electricians can work for themselves and make some great money without a college degree.

How do we learn, anyway? Do we learn by sitting quietly in a class listening to a teacher drone on and on? Or do we learn by doing? Of course, we learn by doing things ourselves, making mistakes, and getting better at them. Yes, a degree might give you options, especially if it's a field where you truly need one, and it might also help open doors. But, your talents, your willingness and desire to learn, and your achievements speak, often, much louder than a degree.

College does have some life benefits, though. It teaches you how to connect with others without mom and dad around, teaches you how to beer bong a beer in 1.2 seconds, teaches you heartache as most have breakups during this time, teaches you how to navigate real life in a bubble of college.

Go to MarkEvansDM.com/MEconomy for the chapter my publisher didn't want in the book.

You've probably also been lied to that your earning potential is greater if you have a college degree. That might have been true in the past, but I don't think it is anymore. Let's look at some of the nitty-gritty numbers.

By my calculation, if a student skips college, they're at least $100 grand ahead of their peers. That's a lot of money, plus avoiding student loan debt (don't get me started). If you're aiming to encourage your kids to think about being an entrepreneur, there's no college degree for that. You don't need to waste your money taking economics courses and advanced algebra. You don't learn what you need to be a successful entrepreneur in college. It's a personality trait and a skill that can be learned. I'd rather see my kids work for a successful entrepreneur for a couple of years in their field of choice and learn by doing what it's going to take them to succeed.

Ask most college students what they're going to do after they graduate, and what answer do you get - I don't know. And my favorite, "I think I'm going to get another degree so I can further my education." It makes me laugh out loud (Lol)!

The truth is, I think most people who go to college aren't sure why they're going. And I think most people who went to college and got a degree know that they didn't need that degree. I mean, let's look at the skills you need in

Go to MarkEvansDM.com/MEconomy for the chapter my publisher didn't want in the book.

business - you need to know how to negotiate, get leads, lead a team of professionals, and build a sales team and foster good relationships. Are these college courses? Maybe. But only in theory. You're not given a chance to negotiate real deals in college. If you're lucky, you'll participate in a simulation.

Most students change their majors multiple times. Why? Because they don't know what they want to do. They haven't lived life yet. They don't know what their true passions and interests are, or if they do, they're not listening to them. To add insult to injury, the majority (about 60%) of college graduates can't even find a full-time job in their chosen field after graduation. It's going to get worse before it gets better.

Degrees just aren't worth as much as they used to be. And I'm not the only one who thinks this. Consider this headline from CNBC (10/13/18):

The future of work won't be about college degrees. It will be about job skills. Truth!

"Formal education will make you a living; self-education will make you a fortune." Jim Rohn

Go to MarkEvansDM.com/MEconomy for the chapter my publisher didn't want in the book.

Chapter 7

The 8th Wonder of the World

My 5-year-old son knows the answer to the question, "What's the 8th Wonder of the World?"

"Compounding Interest!" he yells.

He's right.

I'm sure you've heard about compounding interest and how it is the true secret to making your money grow. But, it's not just about investments. There's a compound effect on every decision you make, either that compounding interest will be positive or negative. Our efforts compound.

Go to MarkEvansDM.com/MEconomy for the chapter my publisher didn't want in the book.

Again, remember you have 100% control over your thoughts, actions, decisions, and what comes out of your mouth. If you eat pizza every day, you'll get fat, and you'll continue to get fat added to fat added to fat. If you eat healthy every day, you'll lose fat, on top of fat, and gain muscle on top of muscle. If you spend foolishly out of already diminished savings, you're taking money away from what you have. If you save and invest regularly, the compound interest or reinvestment of dividends will add money to your money on top of the money you originally invested.

Positive or negative behaviors, when compounded over time, create habits. If you are drinking five beers a day, every day - the compounding result of that is a drinking habit that does not serve your MEconomy. The effect will compound over your lifetime, in general. Poor habits negatively affect your decisions, actions you take, and probably what comes out of your mouth to loved ones and colleagues.

We've talked about success habits and how important it is to hang out with the right people. These are things that compound as well. Staying disciplined, making the changes you need to make, and being the person you need to be create a healthy MEconomy for you and your family. Too many people are just waiting around for someone to fix them or change them. It's up to you to develop good habits. The result of creating good living practices benefits you and those around you, and you'll see the interest compounding very quickly.

Compound Interest as a Life Lesson

I thought I knew what success looked like when I was young. If you were successful, you were just handed things - you floated through life, happy and free (and rich). I thought successful people just hung out at home all day or traveled around the world, flying in private jets to get to their yachts and cared for no one but themselves; they had no problems. But, as I got older and a little smarter, I realized that success is a lot of hard work—a lot of commitment and big decisions. Successful people have problems, too.

It's also too easy to think that a successful person or amazing artist, musician, or dancer is gifted to reach that level of talent and giftedness. They have some unique ability that you or I don't, and that they're born with that gift.

And they do have a gift. But not how I've simplified it. The gift these people possess has absolutely nothing to do with their talent. It has everything, 100%, to do with how much effort, time, and focus they've put into their craft. Take the guitar virtuoso - someone like the late great Eddie Van Halen. Do you think he just picked up a guitar when he was a teenager in Pasadena, could tap the strings and make the sounds that made him famous? No, that took focus, time, and effort. There are no shortcuts.

Side note, Eddie's parents forced him to take piano lessons when he was six. They wanted him to be a classical pianist. Eddie got to be a very good pianist and won many competitions. He is a good example of stepping out to follow his own path and not worrying about what his parents wanted him to do or be. He created an amazing MEconomy around his love for music and improvising.

So, let's take someone who is just learning guitar. They often learn to play a few common chords, and from there, they can put together a few songs. If they're focused and want to learn more, they'll start picking out songs that are a little trickier - including advanced chords and fingering techniques. Moving from chord to chord takes a lot of practice. Picking the strings is much more difficult than strumming. Add in even more advanced techniques like Eddie Van Halen, using both hands to strum, pick, and make chords.

Work and practice build onto themselves. The more advanced skills compound those beginning skills - these skills build one on top of the other. With someone like Van Halen, who taught himself the guitar, his drive and intensity in learning the instrument pulled him far ahead of his peers. He played so that it looked easy - the sign of a true master. His

Go to MarkEvansDM.com/MEconomy for the chapter my publisher didn't want in the book.

success in mastering the guitar seemed to come out of nowhere.

10,000 Hours

"I wish I could play the guitar/paint/dance/sing like ..."

You can! If you want to! Sure, maybe some of us can learn quicker than others, but what separates the guy in the café who knows ten chords and strums to boring folk songs, and someone like Eddie Van Halen is drive - and the compounding effect of learning a craft.

It isn't just me carrying on. There have been studies done on this phenomenon. One study looked at how long it took the great composers to create their masterwork. They looked at the top 500 classical pieces considered masterful by the people who study this kind of thing. These works spanned from 1685 to 1900, so we're talking about a pretty wide sample.

Researchers calculated how long each composer had been composing before creating a particular studied piece. Virtually every one of the great composers had to practice for a decade before writing their masterworks and found success. But, if you hadn't been watching their career from the start, it

Go to MarkEvansDM.com/MEconomy for the chapter my publisher didn't want in the book.

would have appeared as though they were overnight successes.

Through other studies, we know that it takes at least 10,000 hours of working in a field, studying a subject, learning a skill, becoming an expert, or master that skill. It is *compounding effect* at its core. It doesn't happen overnight. You don't practice the guitar once a year and expect to play like Eddie Van Halen, do you? But put in that time, every day, every week, every month, and your skills will build on themselves.

Compounding Interest and Your Finances

The idea of compound interest is known more commonly in the world of finances. You start with an investment, and it grows. That new amount becomes the starting point for additional growth - so the next time it grows, it starts with the original amount, plus that first addition.

Here's a real quick quiz - which would you choose?

I give you a penny doubled every day for just thirty days.

-OR-

Go to MarkEvansDM.com/MEconomy for the chapter my publisher didn't want in the book.

I give you $1,000,0000 cash right now?

What's your choice? $1,000,000 is a lot of money. But, you'd be wrong if you chose that. If I were to double that penny every day for a month, you'd have well over $5,000,000 - $5,368,709.12 to be exact.

Watch what happens to this penny over thirty days!

Day 1	$.01	Day 16	$327.68
Day 2	$.02	Day 17	$655.36
Day 3	$.04	Day 18	$1,310.72
Day 4	$.08	Day 19	$2,621.44
Day 5	$.16	Day 20	$5,242.88
Day 6	$.32	Day 21	$10,485.76
Day 7	$.64	Day 22	$20,971.52
Day 8	$1.28	Day 23	$41,943.04
Day 9	$2.56	Day 24	$83,886.08
Day 10	$5.12	Day 25	$167,772.16
Day 11	$10.24	Day 26	$335,544.32
Day 12	$20.48	Day 27	$671,088.64
Day 13	$40.96	Day 28	$1,342,177.28
Day 14	$81.92	Day 29	$2,684,354.56
Day 15	$163.84	Day 30	$5,368,709.12

But this means you have to be patient - instead of the instant $1,000,000 I'd give you on day one, you'd have to wait a month to realize the benefit of compounding interest. After just 28 days, you've surpassed the $1,000,000 mark.

I know, I know! "Mark, that's not realistic - no one doubles their money every day." I am, though, making this point that compounding interest in life is about being patient

Go to MarkEvansDM.com/MEconomy for the chapter my publisher didn't want in the book.

and consistent over time. That's what creates growth in life and finances.

Time is Your Friend

When I graduated from high school, I had my entire life in front of me. I wasn't focused on anything in particular. I certainly wasn't thinking about retirement! I was living life fast and free - at least, that's what I thought. The truth was, I was investing in bad habits that reversed the progress of my life. Fortunately for me, I had mentors and life teachers, coupled with my eventual drive in life, that helped me focus my vision much further into the future.

I started to make investments. They were small at first. Stocks and bonds caught my eye, and then I looked into real estate. As I made money on one investment - let's say, for example, I made $30,000 flipping a home. I would use that cash to buy a bigger, more desirable house to flip and make $50,000. Each time, I would roll that into the next bigger and better home to bring in $100,000. This would continue for years.

Over time, with focus and a commitment to the process, I was bringing in lots of money. It probably took me about ten years. You might think this was all about investing in properties, but in fact, it was more about investing in myself. On this journey, which wasn't easy, I even almost went

Go to MarkEvansDM.com/MEconomy for the chapter my publisher didn't want in the book.

bankrupt...twice. But I didn't, and didn't quit on myself. Every problem that I overcame was like compounding interest. I would get smarter, faster, and more efficient. The results became dramatically different from when I first started. As time went on, my bank account grew alongside my skillsets.

Coincidence?

The most important aspect of this notion of compounding interest is time. Use it to your advantage.

Time After Time

Let's take a look at brother and sister Lex and Lexi. Neither of them has a lot of money to invest, but Lexi starts investing about $10,000 a year for ten years and then kicks it up to $20,000 for the next ten years. With a (very) conservative 6% annual return. She stops investing by the time she's 44.

Now, Lex, her wild brother, took longer to grow up. He didn't even start investing his money until he was 45 years old. He does the same thing. $10,000/year for the first ten years, then $20,000/year for the next ten years. He stops saving, then, when he's 64 years old. Again, we'll assume a conservative 6% return.

121

Now, they both invested the same amount of money for the same amount of time. A total of $300,000. But, here's the kicker. Lexi stops investing when she's 45, but she keeps that money there to keep building and compounding. By the time she's 65, she'll have more than $1.5 million in her nest egg. Lex? He'll have about $500,000. So, Lexi has 3X the money Lex does at that point.

Lexi has about forty years of growth for her money, and Lex only has twenty. Therein lies the difference. Since Lex started investing much later, he would need to put away three times as much money every year as Lexi did to end up with that much money.

What if Lexi kept investing past the age of 45 and stopped when she was 65? She'd have almost $2.5 million.

It works in reverse too.

Go to MarkEvansDM.com/MEconomy for the chapter my
publisher didn't want in the book.

Credit Cards

Compounding interest in your life and your finances can be your best friend - and time, when you're investing and saving, is your friend. Just the opposite is true if you're spending beyond your means. I don't think there are many things as scary as compounding interest when it applies to debt.

Let's say you're just out of college. You have a brand-new credit card, and you want to travel the world. You don't have any cash, of course. Heck, you don't even have a job in your field. But, hey - you've got that credit card burning a hole in your pocket.

You book that trip to Europe. You're going to take a year off, and you decide before you jump into the workforce. Your parents give you $5,000 as a graduation gift, and you finance the rest of your trip with your credit card. You stay in hostels, and volunteer places in exchange for a place to stay and some food, so you're not spending a fortune. But, at the end of the year, your credit card balance is $5,000.

If you're like me at that age - young and dumb - you just pay the minimum payment. Most of the time, it's about 2% of the balance, for the $5,000, that would be $100 a month. After a year, you'd pay about $1,200 - probably a little more. But, this will give you an idea.

Go to MarkEvansDM.com/MEconomy for the chapter my publisher didn't want in the book.

That's not too bad, right? $100 bucks less per month in your pocket isn't too bad - but, guess what - your original $5,000 is now $5,700 with average credit card interest rates of 15-25%. If you keep paying the minimum, you've given more than $9,000 bucks to the bank, and you will owe more than $10,000.

As long as you keep paying just the minimum, there is no escape. The compound interest is now working against you in the worst way.

The Eighth Wonder of the World

We are who we surround ourselves with within our circle. We are also what we do. If you want to be a millionaire, you have to invest and start as soon as you can. If you're going to be a master painter, you have to paint every day, every week, every month. Those 10,000 hours is no joke. Even if you paint every day for a few minutes or read and learn about painting when you can't get to your supplies, you're still making amazing progress in your life.

Positive compounding interest for health is putting good food in your body, moving and exercising, and taking care of your mental and emotional health. Every day. Every week. Every month. Building habits over time, so it's just natural behavior.

Go to MarkEvansDM.com/MEconomy for the chapter my publisher didn't want in the book.

Negative compounding interest is eating pizza and drinking beer day after day or regularly. You're building a bad habit that turns into a natural behavior - a naturally bad habit.

When you're consistent with small things, over time, that compounds into big things. If you're consistent - you're golden. In the MEconomy, consistency is a choice. You have choices and decisions to make every day. Have a nice healthy meal, or order pizza - again. Go for a walk or sit on the couch playing "just one more" hour of video games. Read an inspiring book or go down the wormhole that is YouTube? Spend your money stupidly, or invest it?

I don't have to tell you what to do. You know what to do. And you have to own up to it - that's the crux, the soul of the MEconomy. It's not my job to "save" you - **you save you**. As long as you are in it for the long haul, and you don't let instant gratification take you by the nose and lead you in the wrong direction, opportunities will keep coming up for you. And you can continue to invest in yourself and your MEconomy.

Nothing will happen overnight. Give it at least ten years.

Go to MarkEvansDM.com/MEconomy for the chapter my publisher didn't want in the book.

Chapter 8

Building and Nurturing Business & Personal Relationships

I don't think there's anything more important to the MEconomy than relationships. The biggest relationship is with yourself. Whether we are talking about our family, friends, colleagues, or customers, relationships are what defines, for most of us, our level of feeling good about our lives. When we have poor relationships, they can overtake our drive and motivation. When we are in positive relationships, we can often achieve far more than we could ever alone.

So, who's responsible for the types of relationships in which we engage? Ourselves and ourselves alone. Through our words, thoughts, actions, and intentions, we can nurture

Go to MarkEvansDM.com/MEconomy for the chapter my publisher didn't want in the book.

important relationships. Like everything else in our lives, we have to find a balance in how we incorporate relationship values in all aspects of our lives, including business/work and our family and friends.

I see people who are incredible at building lasting business relationships - within and outside of their organization. I've also seen those who have burned bridges, creating incredibly destructive turnover rates in employees and customers. It's a recipe for disaster in our business.

Likewise, I see the same for people who are genius at building and taking care of personal relationships. They give to their community and build relationships beyond their inner circle. Of course, I know people who also tend to tear friendships and relationships down. They blame others for their issues and have no real friends - or at least none who are willing to tell them what they think of them.

Take inventory of your relationships. What relationships do you have that you would consider positive? Negative? Do you have more positive or more negative? How are these relationships helping you or hurting you? What are you doing - or not doing - in the relationship that might be compromising its potential? Are you building relationship capital? That's the most important thing.

Go to MarkEvansDM.com/MEconomy for the chapter my publisher didn't want in the book.

Cultivating and Caring for Business Relationships

I'm a business guy, and I've learned the hard way that the success of any business - especially long-term success, lies with the quality of relationships the business or individual has with clients, vendors, and coworkers. I can always be better at this - we all could - and there are some basic things I think we can all do to improve our business relationships.

When you look at the masters of business relationships, what is it that they have in common? What are they doing differently than the Average Joe?

Relationships are about intention, first and foremost. That goes for all relationships - business or otherwise. So when we act deliberately to build and nurture relationships, what does that even mean? Of course, I'm not the first to look at this, so when you dive into the myriad of business books, podcasts, and research, some common traits and behaviors show up.

Change and Adapt

Any good business has to change and adapt with the times. As I write, in the middle of the COVID pandemic, many businesses are adapting and evolving to survive. Mom-and-Pop restaurants are putting together takeout and delivery services. One local restaurant adjusted by opening a cheese

Go to MarkEvansDM.com/MEconomy for the chapter my publisher didn't want in the book.

and wine shop, and they're making a killing. So, too, we have to change and adapt to build meaningful business relationships. We do this by listening to the client - they know what they want, but do they know what they need? When we listen, we're consulting instead of selling. How can you customize or personalize your product or service to deliver much greater value and build long-term relationships with your customer?

Be Present

When you're talking to a client, are you present? Are you really listening? Or are you waiting for the right moment to make your pitch? I've been saying over and over in this book - does it serve you? Does this or that benefit you? Well, you know what? I'll be saying that to your client, too. Does their relationship with you serve them? Are you really there to help, and is the client better off because they know you? Do you know your clients? It doesn't matter if you see or talk to them often. Are you connecting with them? Focus on how you can improve their life and business - and be there - in that moment. Be of service.

Relatability

If you don't connect with your clients, how can you relate to them? At the same time, you might have a very real connection with them, but you may not be able to relate to their needs or wants. My favorite example of this is fitness guru Drew Manning. Growing up fit his entire life, including high school and college athletics, made it easy for him to become a personal trainer. He worked with overweight clients and would get frustrated that they weren't (he thought) doing the program as they should, then complaining to him that he didn't understand what they went through.

Finally, Manning had an 'ah-ha' moment. He realized that he couldn't relate to the difficulties of losing weight and getting fit because he had never experienced that. To better understand what his clients went through, he conducted a personal experiment to gain over 70 lbs. in six months, so he would truly know the challenges of losing weight. He knew that he couldn't truly relate to his clients, so he made it so relating was much easier. He could truly empathize with his clients.

Seeing Things Differently

One of the most difficult things to do in any relationship or situation is to change our perspective. We see things through our own experiences and know-how. But, is that the

Go to MarkEvansDM.com/MEconomy for the chapter my publisher didn't want in the book.

best viewpoint? Usually not. The best view comes from taking a walk in your customer's shoes - that is, understand what your customers are experiencing and feeling, and see how you can adapt to fit their perspective.

Back to Drew Manning again - this is exactly what he did. He literally changed his viewpoint, so he could see what his customers truly needed and wanted. Another example is surveying your customers to see what they might like from your product or service that you're not already giving them. A local restaurant adapted during the COVID pandemic by implementing meal kits so that folks could prepare gourmet meals from their favorite restaurant at home. They only came up with this idea because they shifted their perspective. As a result, they've built and nurtured their relationships with longtime customers.

Stand for Something

More than any time in our modern history, customers demand that their favorite business take a stand - especially if it's unconventional. They want to know what you believe in and why, which makes you multidimensional, and you'll attract clients who feel like you're relating to them. It's easy to be generic, but generic doesn't cut it in today's world.

Go to MarkEvansDM.com/MEconomy for the chapter my publisher didn't want in the book.

Having conviction and standing for something may mean you lose relationships - and keep in mind, you don't have to be an ass to do this. You don't have to take a divisive stance - you can stand for something, though, that most people care about and can unify behind. As you do this, your relationships with your customers will deepen.

The MEconomy in Business Relationships

I'm going to say something that might seem like it goes against the tenets of the MEconomy at first. But hear me out. If you, in your business relationships, think less about yourself than other people, you'll find your relationships more inclined to be loyal and more open.

Sometimes, if you're talking to a client, and you know you don't offer what they need - they need a different product or service - you refer them to that service or product. It ultimately serves you AND your client. They'll appreciate that type of gesture, and I almost guarantee they'll come back to you in the future, and they'll refer others. So, that's how selflessness works perfectly in the MEconomy in this context.

Go to MarkEvansDM.com/MEconomy for the chapter my publisher didn't want in the book.

Be Accountable

There aren't too many more powerful words than "my bad." Accepting when and how you screwed up does more to foster long-lasting relationships with clients than anything else. We all make mistakes, but the bigger mistake is to make excuses or blame someone else. Finger-pointing gets you nowhere. Outcomes do. When you hold yourself accountable in your business relationships, you'll earn respect and gratitude from those around you. Deliver on your commitments and promises, and if you don't or can't, fess up and fix it. NO excuses.

Say What You Mean

One of my biggest pet peeves is when someone is telling me what they think I want to hear instead of what I probably need to hear. If you're consulting on a client's business operations, you owe it to that person to be honest. Tell them what's messed up/wrong about their business. Is this risky? You bet! Being honest and truthful with your clients is how you build trust with your business relationships. This is how you show them *you say what you mean*, and *mean what you say*.

Go to MarkEvansDM.com/MEconomy for the chapter my publisher didn't want in the book.

I challenge you to try these on for size - think about how you can strengthen your business relationships - this includes your organization. Creating a culture that includes the attributes you desire and prioritizes these behaviors will create a place where people will want to do their best work for you and the client. Being honest doesn't only apply to business. It applies to friends and any relationship. Always tell the truth! Don't insult people by telling them what YOU think they want to hear. The MEconomy is about being honest, and it's often going to be a hard conversation. But I promise you; it will result in good relationships in the end.

Nurturing Personal Relationships

Again, of course, I'm not a relationship expert. Like you, I can learn from most of the lessons in this book. Just like business relationships, personal relationships drive our MEconomy. In many ways, we're building our economy FOR the people we care about, our loved ones, friends, and colleagues. So, to me, it makes sense to talk about this in this book. The caveat is that, as always, what works for one person doesn't work for another, and vice versa.

The thing about relationships is they are a living and breathing thing - they change, and they're almost like a separate entity. For instance, marriage involves three different entities: the two partners and the relationship itself. Each

Go to MarkEvansDM.com/MEconomy for the chapter my publisher didn't want in the book.

partner has to take care of themselves, and each partner looks out for the other. At the same time, both partners have to take care of the relationship.

It takes time and energy, and communication to build successful relationships. You can take charge of your relationships, just like you take control of your MEconomy, by putting in that effort - as much as you would put into any other part of your life (if not more). Suppose you see your relationships as entities that need to be taken care of, like a baby. In that case, you'll realize that if you neglect the relationship, you'll often lose it. A big miss in relationships is when people say they want a 50/50 partnership. That's a recipe for failure. You should want a **100/100** relationship. If you're showing up 50/50, it often doesn't end well. Only going halfway is pure laziness. We must level up!

Connect

As we outlined in the section on business relationships, nurturing family and personal relationships is about connection. But when life gets busy, it can become very difficult. One of the Covid pandemic upsides is that, in many ways, we're connecting on a deeper level than ever before - even if we're not in the same room or home. We also see the

Go to MarkEvansDM.com/MEconomy for the chapter my publisher didn't want in the book.

value of our relationships and how critical they are to our emotional wellbeing.

The longest-lived, healthiest and happiest people in the world put their families first, something uncovered by The Blue Zones research I mentioned earlier. The support of your family gives back via support and comfort. In a deep way, connecting with your family means you have to let go of little complaints and spend more time together. You express how much you love each other, every day, in a variety of ways.

Sure, you can tell them. Love can also be expressed just by asking someone what they want to watch on TV, or if they need anything from the store. You can show someone you love them by spending quality time with them - going on a walk and talking (better yet, listening). Simple gifts can go a long way - maybe your loved one saw something they like in the store, and you pick it up for them next time you're out. Want to really show someone you love them? Do something that they love to do, even if you don't. Enjoy that they're enjoying the experience, even if you're not. A quick neck rub or a peck on the cheek can make a nice impact in unexpected moments.

Many of the same things apply to friends - call them and tell them you're thinking of them, or drop a quick email or message. See a little trinket you know they would like? Pick it up for them. Ask them how they're doing, and listen. Call them

Go to MarkEvansDM.com/MEconomy for the chapter my publisher didn't want in the book.

and ask if they need anything when you're going to a store you know they like. Socialize with them, and enjoy the conversation and company.

Friends can become family for us if we're having difficulty with our family. When it's hard to connect with relatives, you make your own family. We get to choose our family, sometimes - and, even though that can come out of a lot of pain, the gift of true friends can be very healing. If you know someone who could use a family, be there for that person, and make sure they understand how you feel about them.

I often send letters to people. It allows me to share my feelings and tell them what they mean to me. To many folks, wait until someone is gone to express how much they impacted their lives. Take a moment right now and write a letter to someone who is still alive and tell them what they mean to you. Pay attention to how it makes you feel.

Be Grateful

Regularly feeling and practicing gratitude regularly to the people you love is a sure way to make your relationships stronger. When you tell someone that you feel fortunate that they're in your life, they feel great, and so do you. It's a type of vulnerability that helps you grow. It can be a quick-expression of thanks - like when you call a friend to talk and thank them for listening. It can be something like saying, "I'm so glad you're in my life." Tell your partner thank you when they ask if you want a cup of coffee.

Practicing gratitude creates closeness and is a sweet expression of affection. Vulnerability equals POWER, contrary to mainstream beliefs. Being vulnerable is strength, not weakness.

Forgiveness

We all hurt others, and we've all been hurt by others. But it's much easier to let go of anger and hurt when you remember that your pain comes from your thoughts and feelings about whatever hurt you. Remember, thoughts and feelings are 100% under your control. **So, when you can face them, you can typically move past them.** I know it's much easier said than done. But it's worth it.

You can't change what's happened in the past. So you have to accept the event and work on distancing yourself from it. If the pain you're feeling is beyond repair with the other person - as in the serious abuse, for example, then you'll have to just move on by yourself. Sometimes you might even have to rebuild/repair your connection with the person. This isn't

Go to MarkEvansDM.com/MEconomy for the chapter my publisher didn't want in the book.

denying the hurt of a specific incident. It's simply a way to normalize it.

Here's why this matters to your life: You will never be able to run fast, make incredible moves, and scale to the person you are destined IF you tied down with a ball and chain. These emotional chains will rob you of clarity. And the inability to be clear-minded will stop you from taking the actions that are required in reclaiming control of your life. You need to figure out a way to forgive the past.

What does forgiveness mean to you? Maybe you think in order to be a good person, you have to forgive others. Maybe you think it's for the OTHER person to benefit only.

But I think, especially in the context of the MEconomy, forgiveness is just as much about **me** - how it can bring me peace of mind and understanding. It's a way for me to find closure. Afterall, that's what counts!

Compassion

Exercising compassion makes us really vulnerable, even if it means pain. I have to tell you; I think this can be the hardest thing to do, especially since it means we let go of all judgment of others. Compassion is something that gets right to one of the first things I mentioned here, communication. It doesn't matter if it's about a friend, a romantic partner, a

139

colleague, or a relative. Compassion is when you realize someone else needs a hand or isn't happy, and you can relate to what they're going through. Again, with no judgment. That's the hard part. It's walking in their shoes. When we show others this, our relationships get even stronger, and when we need compassion, those around us are more likely to give it. Compassion makes the world go round.

Accepting Others

If we're in a healthy relationship (e.g., no abuse), we need to accept others and ourselves - with all our warts, scars, and limitations. We have to accept their bad decisions and even their bad habits. That doesn't mean we have to like them, but they are a separate person from us. How boring would a relationship be if both people were exactly the same in interests, opinions, likes, and dislikes?

We have to be realistic about each other - no one is perfect - I'm certainly not. Just as you accept that about yourself, we have to understand that about those we care for too. If you find yourself struggling with this, it's important to look for the positive(s) in people instead of just the negative(s). We have to understand that people are complex creatures - there's usually much more going on below the surface than we can possibly understand. At the same time, if

Go to MarkEvansDM.com/MEconomy for the chapter my publisher didn't want in the book.

someone is toxic to you and/or taking away from your MEconomy, sometimes you do need to cut them out of your life. You must be willing to not tolerate those people who only drag you down. Being selective of you listen to, whom you associate, and the people who influence your emotional states is imperative in your own MEconomy.

Before you go on deleting everyone, remember it can be a big mistake to see all things as *good and bad* or *black and white* or *right and wrong*. That's just not how the world or people work. <u>You can</u> accept someone just the way they are right now. Humans are complicated creatures for sure. There is a lot to digest. And what I have realized is judgments of others are usually reflections of what we don't like about ourselves. We are our own best critics. Stop putting pressure on yourself and others by thinking there's only one "right way" to do something, think or feel.

Family Life

Don't get the wrong impression, MEconomy is not about taking care of yourself (only) and locking yourself in a room. It's about helping you obtain control so you can take care of you and your family in the best possible ways. If you neglect those you love and those who love you, nothing good

Go to MarkEvansDM.com/MEconomy for the chapter my publisher didn't want in the book.

is waiting for you at the end of that road, I promise you that. People will always try to lie to themselves by claiming to have balance. However, I don't really believe in that word. Life is constantly in motion. Thus, making real balance a lie. What I do believe in is priorities. And family life is a priority to me.

Understanding the principles in this book will show you that you have a role to play. Neglecting your role (in your family) will never strengthen your MEconomy. It will only weaken it. The reason, I believe, has to do with a deep-seeded responsibility that we all obtain at one time or another. Family does that! It gives you a purpose and responsibility like nothing else. When you fulfill that part of your world, things seem to make a lot more sense. Fulfilling my role as a family man helps me understand what is important in the MEconomy. There is no such thing as a balance, but when you know what is important, you will find a way to make the desired results happen. Keep your family a priority.

Social Activities

As I said before, any connection time in your family does not happen by accident. You have to make it happen. The same goes for your friends. If you need to connect with someone because you haven't seen them in a while, you

Go to MarkEvansDM.com/MEconomy for the chapter my publisher didn't want in the book.

need to reach out and not just say, "I need to get together with so-and-so. That's a cop-out.

This is not tough. It can be incredibly easy - like a game night or a special meal every week. Some families love exercising, stretching, or meditating together. How about taking a walk or bike ride together? Instead of watching TV before bedtime, turn the TV off, and everyone picks up a favorite book to read together for 30 minutes before heading off to bed. If you have kids, the older kids might enjoy reading to the younger kids, and vice versa.

Friends can go for weekly walks or share meals at each other's homes regularly. A weekly social-hour, rotating at different homes, is a great way to build a friend ritual. There are now online games that you can play during Zoom calls if your friends or family are far away.

You don't need to spend a ton of money on these activities. I would argue that the less you spend, the more fun and creative your activities become. There are a ton of ideas that you can find on the internet to involve the entire family. Rotate this responsibility. Have weekly family meetings where you share your gratitude, plan activities, brainstorm ideas and solutions to problems you might be having, and give family responsibilities to everyone in the family - you talk as a team, not as parents talking down to the kids.

Go to MarkEvansDM.com/MEconomy for the chapter my publisher didn't want in the book.

If you are like me, you might need to look at it as a part of your business. **Schedule it!** What gets scheduled, gets done. Those who live by the schedule get the results that others only dream. Do you want to make sure you never neglect that part of your world? Mark it down on the calendar weekly.

In a Nutshell

Communication is the key to be treated like we want and treating others in a way that shows love and respect. Whether it's for a business or personal relationship, there are things you can do every day to improve and enhance your relationships.

Life changes - relationships change - goals change. When I was 27, my girlfriend, now wife, and I just wanted to travel the world and see as much as we could see. For seven years, that's what we did. It was fun. It was scary. Sometimes our days were lonely and sad. But, overall, we both look back and know that it was one of the best things we ever did. I grew as a man and as a person.

I knew we would have kids, and we have two beautiful children, Mark III and Dria. We want to make sure we never lose sight of what we want to get out of life and what we want to show them. Life and relationships aren't just about "going through the motions," but deeply connecting and living your best life.

Go to MarkEvansDM.com/MEconomy for the chapter my publisher didn't want in the book.

Chapter 9

Understanding Politics in the MEconomy

First off, I don't care, today or tomorrow, who is President of the United States. I'm going to live my life no matter who's in office, and I'm going to work on making more money and growing my wealth no matter who's in office. I can attest to you that millions will be made with Democrats or Republicans. Focus on MEconomy to get results.

Sure, I have preferences, but the bottom line is that whoever is president is unlikely to affect me personally. Of course, there might be policies that I agree with or disagree with and laws that affect me personally and my business life. But, it doesn't matter. It's my economy that I've created, and if I were to create an economy around who is in the presidential office any given year, I'll eventually fold up and fail.

Go to MarkEvansDM.com/MEconomy for the chapter my publisher didn't want in the book.

These are incredibly divisive times, and I get it. Whether you liked Trump or not, it's clear that he motivated people. Some people would do anything to keep him out of office, and others worked hard to keep him in office. They'd do almost anything, even at the cost of their happiness and living their own life. They'd take on the world and put that weight on their shoulders.

I'm not saying that politics isn't relevant in the MEconomy - of course, it is. Politicians make decisions that will affect you and your business. But, where people make many mistakes, and they overestimate any direct effect that a single politician has on their lives. Even worse, I see people investing tons of time and energy, distracting themselves from developing their personal and business lives.

The problem is that politics and news are EVERYWHERE. It doesn't matter where you live. Unless you spend no time on your computer or phone, except for productive activities like organizing your time and business activities, you're going to get inundated with current politics. Turn on the TV, and even if you're not watching the news, there's politics - right in your face. It's easy to become distracted and stressed - and neither of those serves you.

My advice? Shake it off. Turn off the news. Once you realize the job of the news media is to scare you into watching and obsessing over it, you'll shut it off. And don't be fooled by

Go to MarkEvansDM.com/MEconomy for the chapter my publisher didn't want in the book.

thinking the news media is reporting facts. And watch how much time you spend on social media. You can choose to read about positive things happening globally - no, not just something you think is going your way. Read about true stories of humanity - stories of people overcoming adversity and making life better for themselves and others. Limit your exposure to the garbage flying around, and you'll be happier.

When there is real news going on that we need to know, we still have to be as efficient and focused. So you might need to set aside some extra time to plan accordingly if you're getting a little distracted.

Politics and Kids

In these interesting times, it can feel like we're more disconnected from each other than ever before. I worry about how this time in our lives affects my kids and children across the country. They're seeing and hearing many things that I certainly didn't even think about when I was a kid. How are they being affected by all of this?

Older students are being impacted and experiencing a lot of anxiety around politics and their future. Can you imagine a young teen, or even a pre-teen, even noticing or caring about this kind of stuff? We're just not equipped to deal with it - we don't even really develop abstract, complex thinking

Go to MarkEvansDM.com/MEconomy for the chapter my publisher didn't want in the book.

patterns until we're well into our late teens and early twenties. If we're stressed out and anxious as parents or adults in their lives, it's going to make their life even more difficult.

So, do we shield our kids from this kind of information? I think that would be a huge mistake. Instead, let's talk to our kids about different things happening globally - even difficult topics. We have to let them know that there are different viewpoints and opinions, but we should all focus on what we have in common. In the MEconomy, the objective is to be informed, happy and healthy. When you cut right to the chase, most people share the same wants and needs. Understanding there is a common ground with everyone will yield incredible results.

The secret is to remove the emotion from the conversation. That's when we get into trouble and create unnecessary stress and distraction in our lives. Like normal, civil discourse, we have to listen to our kids and answer honestly (age-appropriate, of course). Let our kids lead the discussion in the direction they need to go.

These days, more and more teens are actively getting involved in politics. It is a great way for them to express themselves. It might not be easy if they're representing an opinion different from our own, and it may not even reflect how they'll think when they're a little older. It can be a source

Go to MarkEvansDM.com/MEconomy for the chapter my publisher didn't want in the book.

of pride or embarrassment for a parent, depending on what your teen is thinking and saying.

But, that's teens for you. We can't, nor should we, try to tell them how to think. How did that go for you with your parents? Kids need to develop their own opinions, and we can show them and teach them how to mine information, so they get all perspectives and sides to the issues that interest them. Politics are very different than values - your kids may develop very different ideas and views than you. That's ok. That's life.

Unfortunately, many parents aren't great models for how to discuss politics in a non-emotional way. I've heard stories of two parents violently disagreeing on political topics. When that happens in front of the kids, it's not just awkward - you're dismantling your MEconomy and letting your anger and stress break down protective walls from the inside. We have to keep our emotions in check, and if we don't, we have to acknowledge that and figure out how to change that type of negativity. Remember, one of the keys to a strong MEconomy is solving problems. Anyone can talk about the problems. Anyone can complain about them. Anyone can disagree with another person. However, the way to strengthen ANYTHING is to be the solution. Train your mind (and your kids' minds) to focus on the solution (NOT THE PROBLEM) at all times.

The life lessons we can teach our kids need to be practical and relatable. We have to prepare our kids to deal

Go to MarkEvansDM.com/MEconomy for the chapter my publisher didn't want in the book.

with tough situations, including getting bullied or harassed about their political views. If we can teach and model how to listen, care about, and have a sense of empathy for others, we can learn to accept our differences of opinion. It really does come down to agreeing to disagree - radicalized views on either side very rarely serve any real purpose, and they certainly won't serve you or your family.

In my discussion about education, I brought up how our education system is designed to keep us in our place, keep us subservient, and train us to be "good employees." I think skills in debating different political ideas is something lacking in our society these days. Most of the time, we're just screaming at each other - sometimes quite literally.

If we can put our egos and opinions aside and teach our kids to question what they're hearing and seeing in the world today, and that means even questioning us, now we're teaching critical thinking. Not every word should be believed verbatim, and the things you dislike because they came from a different view or belief should not be summarily dismissed. We are a country of individuals with varying ideas about what we need in our lives and how we can serve others.

Go to MarkEvansDM.com/MEconomy for the chapter my publisher didn't want in the book.

Moving On

The MEconomy demands that you are aware and informed, but not bothered. Use information about the world to advise and help you strategize. Teach your kids to do their research from a variety of sources. Raise responsible citizens who have the tools they need to pursue their dreams and their own lives well-lived.

We all share similar dreams and goals - we all want the best for our family, community, and country. When we can unite around that, we're building a better MEconomy and contributing to a better world.

Go to MarkEvansDM.com/MEconomy for the chapter my publisher didn't want in the book.

Chapter 10

Your Media Diet

You are what you eat. If you eat crap, your health will be crap. And what you consume and pay attention to in the media will affect every aspect of your life. We consume more media than any other single activity in which we participate. Advertising dollars have pushed media into every part of your entire day. Most of us consume, on average, more than 12 hours of media every day.

What the hell - there are only 24 hours in every day. But, we live in a world where media is everywhere, and our kids have known only this reality. For them, the media onslaught is like water - it's just there, to be consumed. They don't even think about it.

Since media is so prevalent, it only makes sense to make sure we're consuming a balanced diet - otherwise, we'll

Go to MarkEvansDM.com/MEconomy for the chapter my publisher didn't want in the book.

make ourselves very sick. Now, this doesn't mean you have to fast and refuse to consume any media. First of all, that's impossible. This book is a form of media. But, which media calories are empty, and which are nutritious? How much media is too much?

How Much is Too Much?

If it's true that we consume 12 hours of media, on average, is that too much? I think so. Since we can probably agree that much of what we consume is junk food, we can probably agree that some media forms are addictive. Social media, for example. Here, a little goes a long way.

When we are living in our MEconomy, we're controlling everything that we can control. I can choose, for instance, to limit how much time I spend on Facebook or Instagram if/when it starts to interfere with other parts of my life. What I want you to see is not just how much time we use something, but also how we use it. Just because social media can be a drain on your life, it also can be the ultimate tool. Shift your perspective and make it a platform to CREATE rather than CONSUME. Due to the algorithms, we realize the entire platform was built for consumption. So, think differently. Control the time spent. More importantly, control how you use it (for absolute efficiency). Create. Create. Create.

**Go to MarkEvansDM.com/MEconomy for the chapter my
publisher didn't want in the book.**

Do most social scientists recommend we spend no more than two hours on social media a day? Really? That still seems like too much to me. That's two hours of me not being productive, truly educated, and informed. We don't cut out our time on Facebook or other social media, but we can consume much less. Frankly, I think some people are addicted. They spend all hours tweeting or retweeting instead of tending to their job at hand.

You have to find what works for you. If the time spent on social media or with any form of media (healthy or otherwise) is causing problems in other aspects of your life, then you need to consume less. And it's not so much how much we consume, but how we consume media. If you're only consuming things very passively - like scrolling on Facebook and seeing everyone else's perfect life, that can make you sad. When you're engaged and part of a productive community on social media, that can enrich your life.

Another way to figure out how much media consumption is good for you is to look at how you feel after you've had your meal. If you feel anxious, upset, agitated, or any other negative emotion, what you just consumed is not serving you at all. If, on the other hand, you feel relieved, informed, relaxed, or anything positive, you've just had a nice, healthy meal. Pay attention to this as you consume media. Push it away or turn it off if it's not positively serving you.

Go to MarkEvansDM.com/MEconomy for the chapter my publisher didn't want in the book.

When you control what and when you consume media, you will feel better, I see this all the time. People who have stopped watching the news and only read or check things out a few minutes a day tend to be happier and more productive. I never watch TV news and haven't for years now - maybe if it's on at the airport, but that's about it. I especially don't recommend watching the news first thing in the morning. That's like starting your day out by stubbing your toe - instead, you're stubbing your brain!

If someone puts a huge plate of food in front of us, we tend to eat more than we would otherwise. That's the problem with the media now. It's literally everywhere! There's a reason why most of the people who often eat at buffets are overweight and unhealthy. If you sit yourself down at the media buffet every day, you're going to be unhealthy, too. Media manipulates us to want to keep consuming because we naturally are drawn to what gets us riled up - it's exciting - it's adrenalin flowing! And it keeps us watching.

The Media Pyramid

I'm sure you know the food pyramid - there are hundreds of variations, depending on which nutrition or dietary plan you're following. You have to choose the one that works best for you. Again, the MEconomy demands this. But did you

Go to MarkEvansDM.com/MEconomy for the chapter my publisher didn't want in the book.

know there's a media pyramid, too? Like most food pyramids, most of us are consuming way too much junk and media that does not serve us.

At the top of the media pyramid - in other words, what we should be consuming the least, is junk food - highly biased (from either side) junk. This stuff is toxic - like drinking too much or doing drugs. I don't care what your allegiance is in politics. Avoid it!

Just below that are things that also aren't great for us - but not as toxic—social media and news - especially when the news is on in the background all day. My grandma was like this; she had the news on starting from the moment she woke up to the time she went to bed. The news is a dangerous lover. Yes, we can get informed, but remember that news always has an agenda, and it's not to keep you informed. It's to get ratings and advertising money. They also have an agenda to steal your joy, and keep you in fear. You're being manipulated when you watch or consume any more than the most basic amount of news you need to stay informed.

My grandmother lived in fear because of her news consumption. I remember a young boy coming to the door, raising money for some worthy cause - a youth group, maybe. She yelled from the living room, where she was watching the news, "Don't give him anything - I saw on Channel 6 that there are all these scams going on."

Go to MarkEvansDM.com/MEconomy for the chapter my publisher didn't want in the book.

When we live in fear and let the media control us in this way, we are losing out on endless opportunities, and we're making fear-based decisions. If you limit this type of consumption to maybe ½ an hour a day or less, I think you'll be in much better shape and have much less anxiety and worry about your world.

Most of the information we consume, we do so passively. Sitting in front of the TV is a passive activity, while chatting on your phone with a friend or text is more active. So, the next level of the pyramid is interaction-based media consumption. It is interpersonal - interacting with another person or a group. It can be on a Facebook group meeting, a Zoom meeting, or any other media used to communicate with another person or people.

As we move down the pyramid, our media consumption gets healthier and healthier. The next level down is related to participating. That's actively deciding what you want to watch and filtering out stuff that gets you upset. That's good. The key here is still limited since it's not adding too much to your life, but it can be useful. Maybe an hour or two a day.

Where you want to spend more time than less, think about education regarding your media consumption. It is where you're consuming media that is considered generally unbiased or reading to learn. Listening to podcasts that help your personal or business development is productive. You can

Go to MarkEvansDM.com/MEconomy for the chapter my publisher didn't want in the book.

also include reading generally neutral non-fiction books. If you find they are biased, seek out opposing viewpoints and perspectives. Think of this category as the green leafy vegetables part of the food pyramid - it would be hard to consume too much, as long as you're getting what you need to get done every day.

Finally, we get to the bottom of the pyramid, where you should spend the vast majority of your media consumption—talking with friends, attending concerts and museums. This is actualization where you broaden your mind and expand your horizons. The takeaway is this: Connect with your loved ones at a deeper level.

Choose Your Environment

The media is part of our environment. Choose your environment, or your environment will choose you. You're now a follower if you don't take control of your media habit. Just like the food pyramid, you can't survive on eating broccoli alone - you have to combine food to get everything you need to be healthy. When it comes to media consumption, it's the same way. Eat mostly your fruits and vegetables (education and actualization) and get a wide variety in the right amounts. An occasional candy bar or drink isn't going to kill you - but keep yourself grounded and focus on a healthy combination that will improve your mental health and wellbeing.

Go to MarkEvansDM.com/MEconomy for the chapter my publisher didn't want in the book.

Instead of just consuming, let's use our time on media to learn something - whether it's a new hobby, business management, or reading peer-reviewed journals - this is the stuff that makes us happy, and we tend to increase our confidence as we learn more. Podcasts are great for this, too.

THE DM PROJECT
https://markevansdm.com/blogs/podcast

And when we consume actualization media - the kind of activities that help us find and nurture our best selves, we're truly in the MEconomy. These are deep activities that bring great satisfaction to your mind and soul. Deep conversations with loved ones. Art and music that touches you. Give yourself access to a lot of these activities to have a longer, happier life. After all, if you don't deliberately choose where your attention goes, it will be selected for you.

Go to MarkEvansDM.com/MEconomy for the chapter my publisher didn't want in the book.

Don't be a pawn to the media in your life. You have the power and control to consume whatever you want, so choose wisely.

Go to MarkEvansDM.com/MEconomy for the chapter my publisher didn't want in the book.

Final Thoughts

Who do you look up to? Is it someone who you think has everything you want? Or is it someone who is showing you what's possible? I believe that living in your MEconomy helps you reinvent yourself - who you are, what you believe in, and how you want to live your life. You can either improve your life or make it worse - there's no neutral. In my opinion, if an activity is neutral, it's not serving you, and it's a negative.

Every single minute of every single day is under your control. Even if things are outside your direct control, you have 100% control over what you do about it. Get pulled over for speeding? That's under your control. Get stuck in traffic because of a wreck? That's not under your control, and you can either make it work for you or against you. Be thankful you are safe, and instead of fuming and slamming the steering wheel in frustration, pop on a podcast to help you learn more or listen to some relaxing music.

If you take care of the big stuff, all the little stuff will fall into place. Maybe you're familiar with Stephen Covey's famous example of how making a paradigm shift can help you achieve big things - in life and business. In his 1994 classic video, Covey shows how a pile of rocks of all sizes, and even tiny stones, can be fit into a bucket easily.

Go to MarkEvansDM.com/MEconomy for the chapter my publisher didn't want in the book.

He pours a huge back of the pebbles into the bucket, symbolizing all the little things we need to take care of. Covey then challenges a woman from the audience to now fit much larger rocks into the bucket without going over the container's rim. The big rocks symbolize what's truly important in life - important roles and responsibilities, the people we love, self-care, and just our general humanity.

She tries to bury the big rocks into the little stones. She stacks rocks on top of rocks - the audience laughs with her. Covey advises, "By moving some of these little things around, you might be able to squeeze some of the major things in there." And she tries, but there's still not enough room. She tries to pound on one of the rocks, "You know, if it doesn't fit, force it," Covey suggests.

By the time she's got the bucket filled, she's given up her vacation rock and the rock that represents a special time for herself.

Now Covey tells her to take a whole different approach - a different paradigm. Next to him is another empty bucket. She immediately picks up on this and says, "Well, I'd rather put these on the bottom," and proceeds to fill the bucket with all the big priorities that these big rocks represent. They fit easily. She pours the little pebbles in, and everything fits. She hasn't given up vacation, family, time to herself, nor even the urgent matter that one of the big rocks represented.

Go to MarkEvansDM.com/MEconomy for the chapter my publisher didn't want in the book.

I hope this is what the MEconomy helps you see - that we have to take care of the big stuff - the ME stuff. It's not selfish to do so. Our MEconomy consists of those big rocks that Covey introduced more than 20 years ago.

Many of us believe there is a higher power, no matter what we call it. When I was 13, my grandfather was in a nursing home and was declining. We were all in his room when it became obvious that the end was near. He had dementia and had been completely non-verbal for almost eight years. As we were all seated at his bedside, he suddenly sat up, as if the last eight years hadn't happened. He looked around the room and saw my grandmother, his wife, sitting right beside him.

We were all frozen - he hadn't moved in months. But with total awareness and cognition, he looked at his wife, both of them crying, and said, clear as day, "I love you." He laid back down and passed away. I knew then that we are all connected to something bigger than us; however, we define and personalize that.

You know life is fluid - our beliefs are fluid. When we give our power to something bigger than us, we are not giving up control. What we are is giving power to something outside of us - something that provides us with purpose. Without purpose, we have nothing. We're not giving up our own

Go to MarkEvansDM.com/MEconomy for the chapter my publisher didn't want in the book.

power, but we are giving power to that greater purpose. We are connecting with ourselves and that higher power.

A lot of life is about luck. On the morning of December 18, 1867, John D. Rockefeller was running late. He was 28 years old, already pretty successful in the oil industry, and well known in Cleveland. That morning, he was planning on visiting his brother in New York City to check on how his East Coast operations were going.

He rushed to Union Station after saying goodbye to his wife, Laura, and their one-year-old daughter. But, he got to the train a few minutes too late - his bags made it on board, but he missed the train.

It saved his life.

Just later that day, that train jumped the Angola Bridge tracks and fell 50 feet, killing 49 people on board. It burst into flames, passengers were trapped, and many incinerated. Many more were seriously and gravely injured. Later called The Angola Horror, it was one of the worst train wrecks in history.

A couple of days later, after catching a different train, Rockefeller wrote a letter to his wife, expressing his profound gratitude that he had missed that train. It was of no importance that his luggage was lost, as well as the Christmas presents that he was bringing to his brother's family. He had realized, for the first time truly in his life, what mattered the most. His family. His life.

The Angola Horror changed Rockefeller forever, and he, in turn, changed the course of American History.

WTFDYW

I'm a pretty blunt guy. So, I'm going to be very direct with you. My question to you, as you finish reading this book, is: "What the F*** do YOU Want?" Not what you think you want. Not what your mom and dad said you should want. Not what your teachers taught about what to want. What do YOU want?

It's a pretty emotional question, and the answer changes as we change - it changes as we age and live our life.

As you close this book, I want you to do two things. Not for me, but yourself.

First, make a list of what YOU want. Then, make a list of what you DON'T want.

If you struggle with this kind of exercise, you're not alone. I struggled with this for years. Very few people know what it is that they really want. Even now, after so many years, I still catch myself losing sight of my MEconomy.

You have the choice to be the victim or the victor. You can live the life you want. Even if you're not there, yet - you can walk that path by claiming and protecting your MEconomy. That realm is where your energy has the most value and best spent. That's where it matters the most. That's what you have 100% control of.

The most important thing to remember is that you get to choose what the next "page" in your life looks like. YOU DO! Not your friends, not the TV, not society, not the neighbors, not your co-workers, not your past, and certainly not the government. YOU. When you understand the principles in this book and apply them, you will begin to understand how much control you have over the next phase of your life. Connections and solutions will appear. You'll deepen relationships with the ones you love. Your bank account will expand, your business will grow, your circle will become full of high-value individuals, and your life will start to look like those posters you had on your wall when you were ten years old.

Sounds amazing right? Well, here is the best part --- Your newly formed "MEconomy" will live on throughout your family forever. Your kids will see what control really looks like. They will adopt the same principles. And they will embrace the rewards of your *shift* for as long they too adhere to the MEconomy rules and keep their hands on the steering wheel.

Go to MarkEvansDM.com/MEconomy for the chapter my publisher didn't want in the book.

Your family (and friends) will see how much you evolved, which will help guide them to a more fulfilled life as well. Ultimately, you set the example for all others to duplicate. Yes, this book is certainly about you, your mind, your dreams, your actions, and your beliefs. But let's make no mistake about it, your *MEconomy* is really all about them. The MEconomy is really about the FULL picture - **YOU and THEM**. What you do right now will affect those around you positively or negatively.

Your legacy is completely reliant on what you do next. Whatever you do, just remember **YOU** are in control of your **MEconomy.**

Go to MarkEvansDM.com/MEconomy for the chapter my publisher didn't want in the book.

Thank You

I appreciate you investing the time to read MEconomy as this will change your life for the better if you implement it.

I care about your success and would love to hear about your journey.

Please keep me in the loop by going to my social media, following me, and messaging me. My handle on all platforms is @markevansdm.

I do personally reply to all messages.

I'm honored to be on this journey with you and I trust you'll use these principles to improve your MEconomy.

It's now time to get to work!

PEACE!

Go to MarkEvansDM.com/MEconomy for the chapter my publisher didn't want in the book.

Other books by Mark Evans DM

(Available on Amazon)

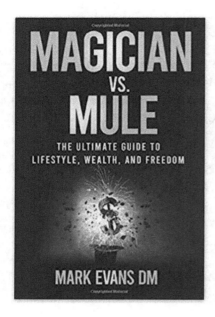

Magician Vs. Mule

We all want to become successful in life. However, how we all go about doing it is different from person to person. What I have learned throughout my journey is that there are two kinds of people: Magicians and Mules. Success was unattainable until I was able to shake out my mule mentality and become a magician.

That's when it all clicked. This book will show you how to do the same. Have you been working way too hard for your entire life and not seeing any of those financial dreams come to fruition? Maybe you are a mule. Don't worry, you can always change. There's always a little magic in everyone. It's time to dig down deep and find it. This book will show you how Mark Evans DM is a 9 time bestselling author. He's the creator of innovative, cutting-edge software; he's an expert in teaching business owners how to automate and scale their business; and he coaches business owners around the world on how he runs two 8-figure businesses with his 10 Minute Business Owner strategy.

Go to MarkEvansDM.com/MEconomy for the chapter my publisher didn't want in the book.

The 10-Minute Business Owner: Experience Freedom, Build Wealth, and Create a Life Worth Living

Are you a business owner that's working harder but not making more? More stress, less sleep, and you still rarely get to spend time on yourself and family? If you and your company are really ready to thrive, it's time to begin working on your business, not in it.

Mark Evans DM spends only ten minutes a day on each of his two multi-million dollar empires. In The 10-Minute Business Owner, he shares with you how to work less and make more, while maintaining control, visibility, structure, and culture. From pushing boundaries to getting focused, hiring right, and knowledging up, Mark offers high-level advice to growing wealth and freedom. Spending your entire life with your business doesn't make you a better leader. Stop wasting time, start thinking bigger, buy back your time, make more money, and discover what success truly is.

Go to MarkEvansDM.com/MEconomy for the chapter my publisher didn't want in the book.

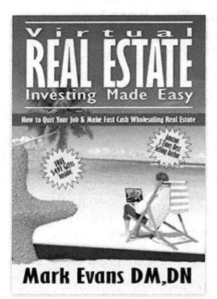

Virtual Real Estate Investing Made Easy: How to Quit Your Job & Make Fast Cash Wholesaling Real Estate

This is a great book to learn how to become a virtual real estate investor. These are the same lessons that allowed me to do deals and get my business rolling. I really can't say enough about Mark Evans DM.

He has helped me in so many ways to get my business going in the right direction. The tools are here in this book to help you become virtual. Sometimes, taking that first step is the most difficult to do. Taking action is the crucial part. Then continue to implement and keep moving forward to success.

Go to MarkEvansDM.com/MEconomy for the chapter my publisher didn't want in the book.

CPSIA information can be obtained
at www.ICGtesting.com
Printed in the USA
BVHW091343210621
610125BV00014B/2939/J